A Time to Wake Up

Carla Jo Holland

ISBN: 1463565607

ISBN-13: 9781463565602

A special thanks to my lovely friend Gail Pommerening for allowing use of her artwork for the cover of my book.

Thank you, Father Shroud, for giving me permission to reprint part of the works of Anthony de Mello.

DEDICATED TO THOSE THAT LISTEN.

Deep listening is miraculous for both listener and speaker. When someone receives us with open-hearted, nonjudging, intensely interested listening, our spirits expand.

—Sue Patton Thoele

Acknowledgement

I am grateful to my many clients, co-workers, and friends who shared their stories with me. Out of respect for their privacy, names and genders have been changed, along with all identifying details, while preserving the spirit of their stories.

A special thanks to Derek Mazula for his editing skills, support, and relentless patience. I am also grateful to Bernette Finley Drawe, Lois Kreidermacher, Bill Hedberg, my niece Haley, and my sister, Kim, for reading through drafts and providing support. A warm thanks to Henk and Nerida De Jong for taking such good care of me while I wrote my first draft in a rare snowstorm in Saint-Cirq-Lapopie, France.

And finally, Marcia, for listening to me.

CONTENTS

Preface. xi

Section One – How We Fall Asleep. 1

Chapter 1 – Early Childhood Decisions 3

Chapter 2 – Influence of Addictions. 21

Chapter 3 – Deprivation and Parental Functioning 31

Chapter 4 – Childhood Roles .41

Section Two – Waking UP. 51

Chapter 5 – Identifying Patterns in Relationships 55

Chapter 6 – Humility Lost and Faound 65

Chapter 7 – Boundary and Identity Development. 73

Chapter 8 – Shame and Self Identity 91

Section Three – Staying Awake. 109

Chapter 9 – Differentiating Spirituality and Religion. . . .113

Chapter 10 – The Tools 123

Chapter 11 – Intimacy and Relationship Skills 137

Conclusion – Expanding Choice and Freewill. 145

Bibliography. 149

The mass of men lead lives of quiet desperation. What is called resignation is confirmed desperation.... A stereotyped but unconscious despair is concealed even under what are called the games and amusements of mankind.

—Henry David Thoreau, *Walden*

Preface

I do not understand my own actions. For I do not do what I want, but I do the very things I hate.

—Romans 7:15

People often come in for therapy seeking the answer to this or a similar question, "Why can't I do better when I know better?" They are unable to see that there is quite a difference between the knowing and the doing. I see this in addicted individuals who know that eating donuts or consuming alcohol or continuing harmful behaviors is destroying them, yet they cannot stop these destructive actions. I also see it in individuals who know that yelling at their children or spouse is hurtful, yet continue to periodically do that which they do not want to do.

Education or information represent the critical first step in the initial phase of "knowing". Knowledge gets us to pay attention in the first place. Yet knowledge alone will not bring about lasting changes in entrenched behaviors. Sometimes knowledge actually intensifies the behaviors we are trying to eliminate. This is especially true in those behaviors fueled by insecurity or feelings of shame. Sometimes insight only serves to strengthen both self-loathing and unproductive behaviors when we realize the fuller consequences of our actions. Negative behaviors (like losing one's temper or acting out) serve to temporarily medicate and numb the growing self-dissatisfaction, which creates a powerful spiral of destruction.

In many religions, the answer to Paul's struggle in Roman 7, is to "surrender the flesh to the spirit." In twelve-step programs it is to enter the process of acceptance that comes after admitting our powerlessness over some behaviors or intrusive thoughts. In Eastern philosophies it is the process of becoming less attached to the things of the earth.

In order to change behavior, we need to have a deeper awareness of the behavior. This goes beyond early knowledge and understanding and looks at the reasons we chose the behavior in the first place. The word chose is an interesting one because many would say that these behaviors were not actually chosen but simply happened as they always have. Getting to this deeper understanding (whatever religious, cultural, scientific, or philosophical belief we align ourselves with) is most often a process and not a single event.

I chose to write this book for two reasons. The first is that the process of awareness is often overlooked. Many seek distracting shortcuts or today's newest tool for enlightenment in their search for an immediate change. This has created a plethora of commercial New Age products and perspectives. I, along with many of my clients and friends, have been enticed to sample and experience some of these methods. Though entertaining and intriguing, these products or methods alone seldom bring about greater spiritual maturity. The second reason I write this is that the process of awareness or enlightenment (or waking up) is not out of reach to those of us who cannot sign up for a year in a Tibetan monastery or three days a week of psychoanalysis. It is a fairly straightforward process that I have had the opportunity to witness over the years with my clients. It is a progression of insight and understanding that leads to greater compassion toward oneself and others. This is humanity at its finest.

SECTION ONE
How We Fall Asleep

> I know over half of what I perceive as reality is an illusion of my own making. I just don't know which half.
> —Carla Jo Holland

We may fall asleep to ourselves and our full potential by exchanging our need to develop our essence and character for our need to feel safe and defended from harm. As children we have very few choices in seeking safety if our environment is not secure. Deprivation of essential resources in the family such as security, acceptance, nurturance, and structure are the primary reasons we unconsciously –"choose"- defenses over our development. Sometimes we construct defenses and roles to keep us safe instead of forming our identity. By identifying some of the defenses and role patterns we may have developed to cope, we begin to clear away the distortions that keep us asleep.

Many of our perceptive lenses, which determine how we later view the world and reality, were shaped by reactions and experiences we had as little children. If we had a nurturing and safe childhood, most likely the lenses with which we view life will give us clear vision. However, if there was not a sense of security and acceptance, the lenses may be smudged. Cloudy lenses from childhood can impair our judgments of reality and ourselves as we grow. How often do you find yourself needing to clean your glasses? Self-examination can give you clear lenses, which provide even better vision than clean glasses.

The reason this is such good news is that there has also been a shift in our cultural lifestyle that further deprives the family of additional resources. We, as a society, receive less support from the formerly solid structure of extended family and community. Many of my clients describe overwhelming feelings of isolation, loneliness, and anxiety. In response, we're developing ever more methods to defend ourselves from such feelings. Increasingly we develop methods to defend ourselves from such feelings. In the face of all this, many of us exhibit uncompassionate or unacceptable behavior toward ourselves and others.

This section will help you identify some of the factors that prompt children to create protective defenses rather than to develop their unique self. By increasing our awareness of our past decisions, we become better able to clearly choose our future. We cannot change the events of the past, but we can change how our past affects our present and future.

CHAPTER ONE

CHILDHOOD DECISIONS

Though I diligently sought them, there are
no shortcuts or paths leading to awareness or enlightenment or simply changing
my behaviors that do not include rigorous
self reflection and forgiveness of what is
found.
— Carla Jo Holland

EARLY DECISIONS AND LASTING IMPLICATIONS

I am amazed by the many decisions we make in
response to life and relationships before the age
of sixteen. We make many before the age of six!
All of these decisions contained some elements of
wisdom. Given that you are reading these words
today, those decisions kept you both alive and
engaged in the process of seeking greater self-
awareness. Most of our childhood perspectives
and decisions are deeply imprinted within us and
remain throughout adulthood as rules for living.
Psychologists call these our *transference issues*.
Some of these decisions you may remember making; many you will not. This is why it can be difficult
to change behaviors without understanding why
we made the decision in the first place. It is difficult

to change any policy or rule in life without understanding the original intent.

I do not remember making my decision to be terrified of heights, but based on my behavior, I know it was a strong one. After forty-plus years of being restricted by this decision, I decided to examine it as I prepared to drive through the Rocky Mountains. Previously I had either avoided the mountains and most heights or become ill attempting to travel in them. Just thinking about climbing my ladder to clean out the gutters created great anxiety!

As I climbed a steep grade on this particular mountain drive, I remembered the voice of my rather horrified mother telling my father to grab me before I fell into the canyon. I recalled being four at the time and in awe of the edge of the cliff as I ran toward the rim to get a better view. I decided at that point in the drive to shift out of my emotional state and become more of an observer of my reactions. This transition was like parenting a small child. Many of us can set powerful emotions aside to step in and assist someone else. However, the chemical power of fear and injured self-worth makes it harder to parent ourselves. In this case my detached view kept me calm as I reminded myself, "This is a memory, these are old feelings, and you will not fall." I realized that I had made the decision to be terrified of heights at a very young age for some good reasons that no longer exist. As an adult I am a little less impulsive and know better than to run toward a canyon cliff. Again, I still have some physical reactions to heights, such as dizziness, but they diminish every time I take a mountain hike. I have examined my decision regarding heights and adjusted it based on what I know today compared to what I knew at the age of four.

My decision regarding heights was a fairly minor one. Other decisions before reaching adulthood that may have far-reaching consequences. For example, I and others have had difficult first-love relationships. Mine ended with my high school sweetheart deeply betraying me during a particularly vulnerable time for me. I was away attending a funeral for one of my immediate family members. Because both my emotional reserves and my support system were already overextended, I made some dramatic decisions to cope on my own out of both the grief and betrayal. I decided that it was very painful to trust people, and I kept myself emotionally distant from most others for years. This had far-reaching consequences on the quality of my subsequent romantic relationships and first marriage.

Betrayal by a first love does not always lead to such a dramatic response. Our coping responses depend on our available external and internal emotional resources. These reactions can range from cautious care in selecting a partner to reckless negligence in entering relationships. The latter choice reinforces the original injury.

We make many decisions early in our life that can affect our awareness more deeply. We often make profound decisions, before we are out of child-hood, about whether this world is a safe and loving place with areas of danger, or a frightening and hostile place with areas of safety. What decision did you make at the age of six about the quality of life? What decision did you make at sixteen or eighteen about the quality of love? What were the reasons for these decisions?

Is the world safe and loving? The answer we come up with and our resulting decision sets the tone of much of our life! If we approach life as hostile, we will develop powerful coping mechanisms that usually include equally powerful defenses and, perhaps, addictive behaviors in order to feel safe. Such a decision can cause anxiety, depression, and other mood disorders. Who enjoys living in a fearful world?

ADAPTIVE AND MALADAPTIVE BEHAVIORS

Depending on our temperament and external resources as children, we choose several ways to adapt and survive even the most horrific situations. This adaptive behavior keeps us alive and sane. Nevertheless, it becomes what psychology calls *maladaptive behavior* when the situation no longer warrants such behavior. The book, <u>Sybil,</u> by Flore Rheta Schreiber, illustrates extreme maladaptive behavior. In the story a child develops sixteen personalities in order to cope with torture by her mother. Sybil's childhood home, a white house, still stands on the edge of town, five miles from my house. Some believe Sybil was fictional. She was not, nor is the many clients I have seen, who developed similar coping mechanisms in response to indescribable childhoods.

Not all cases are this extreme. I have worked with over a half dozen clients who require the noise (not the circulating air) of an electric fan in order to fall sleep. They all described finding the fan to be the most effective white-noise machine available to them as children. The fan would help them drown out their parents' fighting, or their dad falling down as he made his way to bed intoxicated. It would help them block out the scary sounds of their home at night. This was adaptive and resourceful behavior on the part of these clients. It only becomes maladaptive or problematic when they cannot sleep without the fan as adults in a safe and quiet homes, hotels, or tents. Can you see the restrictions some of your adaptive, childhood choices may have brought to your adult life?

I regularly facilitate classes on developing creativity. The primary purpose is not to teach something new, but to unlearn some of the messages we may have accumulated over the years regarding the worth of our art. Many of my participants report one or two negative comments or events from their adolescence, which prompted their decision to turn their back on their artistic or creative talents. This is a particularly meaningful subject for me. I stopped painting and drawing for several years after junior high, despite being told by my art teacher that I had exceptional talent. He seemed to be attracted to me and often whispered "artistically suggestive" comments in my ear. Because his behavior was subtle and confusing, I did not report it to my family or principal. Later I came to understand that the impact of it was not so restrained as I had been in my response. At age fifteen I had made two decisions about my art. One was that I really had no talent, but was rather attractive to this teacher. The second was to stay away from art teachers and art! Twenty years later, after evaluating, these decisions with more awareness, I once again picked up my paintbrush.

Adaptive behaviors can also originate later in life. Dramatic examples in adult adaptation were observed in the prison camps at the end of the World War II. Despite the assurance of the Allied troops, many prisoners refused to walk through the open gates to freedom. Their adaptation to prison suddenly had become maladaptive.

I worked with a man in his late forties who came in for help after a difficult marriage and divorce. He was a hard-working and successful businessman. His wife had secretly drained most of their life savings and given it to a "faith-healing church" as he called it. He felt he had only a few pieces of original and valuable sculptures to show for his years of hard work. He thus became highly protective of these artifacts and went to great lengths to guard them, which included elaborate security systems. His attempts to protect himself from further theft became problematic when he began dating again. He refused to let the woman he was dating into his house, afraid she would steal the sculptures or only marry him to take his valuables.

He was able to reduce these restrictive behaviors once he stopped focusing on his ex-wife. As he began to examine the emotional injury of her theft, he saw that he had inadvertently linked his worth and value as a man with the loss of his assets. Increased awareness enabled him to reevaluate his worth based on his internal assets. His ex-wife had taken his money, he realized, but she could not take his self-worth.

In my class on family of origin issues, I tell a humorous adaptation story called "Holiday Ham." My class co-facilitator always holds her breath when I begin the story because I have yet to tell it without leaving out some small but key element. My refusal to read from my notes is clearly my maladaptive denial of my growing farsightedness.

"Holiday Ham"
Julie and her newlywed husband Paul were in the kitchen preparing Easter dinner where her extended

family had all gathered for the holiday. Julie placed the full ham on the counter and chopped off one-third of it. She then went to the kitchen window and tossed the third of the ham out the window after saying a brief prayer to the animals of the world. Paul was shocked by this behavior and asked, "What are you doing?"

Julie simply stated, "It is a Lutheran custom to say a prayer while offering a third of the Easter ham to the animals." Paul told her he had never heard of such a thing despite knowing several people of the Lutheran faith. Julie suggested he ask her mother, who was in the living room, for additional details on this Easter ritual.

Paul went to the living room and asked Julie's mother Ruth about the ritual. She replied, "Oh, yes, we must give at least three inches of the left end of the ham to nature through an open kitchen window. I think the prayer is optional."

Paul asked Ruth, "Why do you do that?" Ruth stated she was not sure where the Lutheran custom originated, but was sure her mother, whom they called Granny, would know.

Paul then went off to find Granny sunning herself on the patio. "Granny," Paul asked, "Please tell me about the Lutheran ritual of cutting off a third or three inches of the Easter ham and giving it to the animals with or without a prayer. Neither your daughter nor granddaughter seems to know the origin of the tradition." Now Granny was a religious woman and an elder in the Lutheran Church, so surely she would know the reasons behind this ritual, Paul reasoned.

Granny thought for a while, then a smile came to her face. "Paul, I do not know of any sort of Lutheran Easter ritual, but I do know I would often find my large Easter ham too big for my favorite baking pan, so I would chop off a few inches and throw it out the window for the animals, so it would not go to waste. Sometimes, I would feel selfish throwing good meat away, so I would say a quick prayer. Ruth must have seen me do it several times when she was young. She always helped me in the kitchen."

Many such rituals evolve as adaptive behavior that becomes maladaptive when something like a bigger pan is found and the original reason for the ritual is lost. Do you have any such rituals in your family? Do you maintain defenses that may be no longer necessary?

With an understanding of adaptive and maladaptive behaviors, we can go back and review the family we grew up in from the perspective of the resources that were available or not available. We then can explore the origins of some of our behavior patterns and make conscious choices as to whether they are still necessary or not.

FAMILY RESOURCES OR DYSFUNCTIONAL FAMILIES

Focusing on resources within ourselves and our families, whether they were available or denied, often yields significant insight into our behaviors. Resources important to children go well beyond food, clothing, shelter, safety, and security. They include emotional support, nurturance, structure, and acceptance.

Many of my clients describe growing up in a dysfunctional family as "learning to survive" rather than "learning to live." The label *dysfunctional* is not especially helpful by itself in leading to increased self-awareness. Labeling one's family as dysfunctional can sometimes minimize our sense of responsibility for our behaviors, instead of leading us to deeper understanding. It also may not be helpful in reducing judgments and blame. These two defenses can prevent us from assuming individual responsibility necessary for growth. Reviewing our childhood experiences from the perspectives of resources and shortages reduces the need to activate defenses we may have developed. We then can focus energy on examining our adaptations, related behaviors, and thoughts. Energy focused on increasing our perspective and understanding is generally much more fruitful than expanding energy on judging others.

I have seen another misuse of the dysfunction label in the situation of a man named Lee. The first therapist Lee saw for individual counseling during a transition in his life was more concerned with investigating the origins and specifics of his dysfunctional family than addressing Lee's broader underlying issues. Lee finally said to his therapist, "I have enough to deal with during this transition and do not want to add the stress of defending my family from your judgment." Hearing his family labeled as dysfunctional created a defensive backlash in him toward therapy and self-examination that lasted for quite some time.

I've seen numerous examples of grown children of alcoholics who believed they became alcoholic themselves due to their family's dysfunction. This is only a partial explanation for their compulsive use of alcohol, one that provides very limited insight or understanding of their decisions and choices then and now.

Once these clients began to examine their family in terms of resources, they are able to more accurately assess the areas of deprivation that led them to choose certain coping mechanisms such as drinking. I worked with a woman who could not understand why she woke up in the middle of the night with an overwhelming drive to consume large quantities of food. She explained the behavior as related to growing up in an alcoholic and abusive family. This level of insight did little to change her behavior.

When she began to explore the lack of any safety or security she felt at night, when her father came home violently intoxicated, she began to make progress. She was able to understand that the powerful level of fear she felt at these times drove her to seek some way to cope. At five, she was internally limited in her ability to cope, so she chose food to comfort her fears. At thirty-five, once she understood, on both an emotional and intellectual level the reason for her choice, she was free to choose other responses to her middle-of-the-night waking.

Cultural Shifts in the Family

We are witnessing an unprecedented expansion of options and opportunities across the globe. This expansion may not be having an optimum effect on the quality of our relationships both within and outside of our families. In our search to expand our resources, we may become spread too thin and actually distance ourselves from relationships and emotional resources that are right next door. To many people's surprise, they find they have more ways to be in contact but feel less connected.

I remember meeting a woman at a local fundraiser who had recently come over from the UK with her young daughter and husband. She stated she felt very isolated during the day in their apartment and spent significant time on the internet, emailing friends and family back home. When she told me where she lived, I had to smile. I had lived in the same complex with an infant more than twenty-five years ago. Since I had no internet, I talked to just about everyone I saw in the hallways, in the elevator, in the mailroom, and in the laundry room. I was more than a little lonely and homesick. The apartments were made up of elderly folks wanting to be close to downtown as well as medical students and professionals wanting proximity to the local hospital.

I shared with her that not since college had I felt such a community of support as in that complex. The elderly women just loved watching my baby boy while I ran errands. The students and professionals usually had some time in the evening to drop over for a game of cribbage or some home-cooked food. She quickly got the idea and soon built a nice support system for her family.

It has been interesting to observe how the dramatic changes in our culture have contributed to restructuring of the extended family. As our population has shifted from rural family farms to small communities to large industrial cities to remote technological communities on the internet, our family of support has become smaller. Having extended family members nearby or living in a close knit community provided a wealth of security and alternative resources, if one or both of our parents became impaired, or if the family ran short on resources.

An acquaintance of mine, Mary, described her large farm family in such a way. "Even though Mom was mentally ill and probably had severe postpartum depression, Grandma was always there in the rocking chair offering her lap to anyone who wanted to take time to sit. Her comfort saved me, I think. At the least it saved my self-esteem. Mom was too sick and too self-absorbed to care about what I was doing, but Grandma always had time for me."

What a resource, to have more than one or two people to go to for support and comfort! How many people did you have to go to for emotional support when you were growing up? If you did not always have people there for support, how did you cope or adapt to your feelings and thoughts?

Our family size has also decreased dramatically over the years. Many people did not necessarily consider their siblings a strong source of emotional support growing up, but rather a force to be overcome until adulthood. However, siblings, even when they do not particularly get along, can provide a wealth of emotional support in terms of building self-reliance. Through the childhood struggle and support, along with the comfort of sharing a bedroom or a bathroom with siblings, many of our social coping skills and positive ways of adapting are formed. We also may feel a sense of mastery in the process of successfully quieting the youngest one in the room after a bad dream.

Following one Thanksgiving with my family, I volunteered to take my nieces home with me for the long weekend. Julia was seven, Lizzy was five, and Sara was two. They camped out with my daughter in her bedroom. The first night Sara woke up screaming from bad dream. My daughter quickly led her into my room for help. Sara and I then had a two-a.m. discussion in my bed on "Who tells the angels what to do?" After she was satisfied with our conclusions, Sara fell fast asleep. The next evening my daughter was out of town, so the girls slept in her bedroom without her. I got a full night's sleep. The next morning I asked the girls how they slept. Julia and Lizzy both said they were woken up by Sara crying. I asked them why they did not come and get me. Both beamed with pride as Julia said, "Auntie Carla, we got her back to sleep all by ourselves." Sara was smiling as well, so I did not ask how they accomplished such a daunting task in the middle of the night. It appeared to me that all three had experienced a greater sense of reliance and accomplishment.

What support did you receive from your siblings? What social skills did they teach you?

Paradoxically, having more external resources than our ancestors has both created and reduced opportunities for self-esteem building in our families. It would be difficult to question your value and worth as a child if your chore was to feed the family that night or keep the fire going on a brutally cold evening. Just two generations ago, children were often essential for the survival of the family on many levels.

Children are often optional for the functioning of families today. Unless we are creative as parents, it is difficult to give a child the sense of worth derived from doing indispensable tasks. The number of essential or indispensable tasks just isn't that large, when so much convenience is right at our fingertips. But there are a large number of small tasks that we can ask our children to help out with. Sure, it takes time to both generate and follow up on the chore list, but I can more easily find the motivation to do this when I remember the satisfaction of having helped make a dessert that my parents complimented me on at dinner. Or the sense of accomplishment I felt at having cleaned windows that were caked with dirt. And while I sit here today as a middle-aged parent, it is not hard for me to remember that I was reluctant to do some of these chores, as I always had better things to do. But secretly, after I had done the work, I gained an enhanced sense of self-esteem and self-efficacy.

Some of the benefits or advantages we give our children may deserve closer examination. I will sometimes err on the side of withholding luxuries rather than overindulge my children's immediate wants and desires. I do not mean to bypass the often challenging responsibility of determining what my children need versus what they want in order to thrive.

To determine what a child needs, we watchfully factor in their developmental stage, their personal temperament as well as their ability to take responsibility and use other resources. The reward for this sometimes time-consuming task is a self-disciplined and secure child. Imagine a child who comes to you and says, "I am sixteen now and I need a car to drive to school." Yes, developmentally this child has the skills to drive, but does he or she have the maturity to responsibly manage a car? What about the ability to contribute to the upkeep either in finances or commitment? Will having a car contribute to his or her primary task of doing well in school? These basic questions help determine a need from a want. You can also use them to promote delayed versus instant self-gratification. When my child needs a new video game or the most in-style shoes, the questions usually reveal that these things are actually wants, which require planning and investment to own.

It helps if we have an understanding of how self-discipline functions within ourselves to determine our children's wants from needs. How do you determine your wants from your needs? What do you do when your wants conflict with your needs?

Yes, some issues of entitlement can arise out of extreme family deprivation, but most come from over-indulged children who have not had the opportunity to distinguish between what they need versus what they want and to delay the gratification of the latter.

Most parents are loving, generous, and well intentioned with regard to their children. However, they get little guidance on how to navigate the recent shift in resources that we now have to simultaneously offer and withhold from our children. Awareness of a child's needs versus what they want can be a helpful tool.

Does your desire to compensate for the past influence your common sense and perspective in parenting both your children and yourself?

CHAPTER TWO
INFLUENCE OF ADDICTION

The purpose of man's life ... is to become an abject zombie who serves a purpose he does not know, for reasons he is not to question.
—Ayn Rand

NATURE OF ADDICTION

Addiction is a powerful force capable of consuming both the awareness and free will of those who unintentionally succumb or surrender to it. I use the word *unintentionally* as I have yet to meet any addict who deliberately set out to become enslaved or give up their power to anything or anyone.

Succumbing to addiction does involve a choice of sorts, although one that is not very conscious. From my observations, people surrender to addiction by choosing to relieve their unpleasant thoughts and emotions with the fastest, most effective manner available. This is one of those few choices that often cannot be undone for both physical and, possibly, genetic reasons. A considerable amount of research over the years has examined the genetic factors involved in addiction. Even though I am aware of no scientific evidence of a gene that promotes addiction, mounting evidence suggests that genetic factors may increase susceptibility to it.

To further understand addiction it is helpful to understand the view of addiction as a disease commonly accepted in this country. The disease concept of alcoholism was accepted by the American Medical Association in 1956. This concept revolutionized both the view of alcoholism and how it is treated. It has not been particularly effective in reducing the stigma of addiction, but then the model has only been around for fifty years, while the judgment of addicts as weak-willed, hopeless, immoral characters has been with us for thousands of years. This stigma has had a significant impact on discouraging people from seeking help for their addiction.

I have often seen the disease concept of addiction misunderstood and misinterpreted by both addicts and their family members. Labeling a set of symptoms as a disease does not remove or reduce an individual's responsibility to manage their disease but actually enhances it. Those newly diagnosed with diabetes do not have greater permission to eat whatever they prefer, but rather greater awareness of the consequences of not managing the disease by changing their lifestyle. Thus diagnosing addictions as a disease process enhances a person's responsibility to recover by identifying the specific affliction and its very predictable and deadly nature.

The simple description of addiction is "the overwhelming urge to use a substance or a behavior for relief." Process- or behavior-related addictions include: workaholism, shopping, gambling, sexual compulsions, or just about any habitual, self-destructive behavior that relieves stress. The most vulnerable are those who grew up in stressful or chaotic homes without effective modeling of healthy coping mechanisms.

What coping skills were you taught as a child to reduce stress? Are you vulnerable to a process addiction?

A man named Jerry came to me for help with his gambling addiction. His accountant informed him that he had tallied losses of more than one-hundred-thousand dollars in a local casino and handed Jerry my card. I liked Jerry immediately as did most people who met him. He was a hard-working man in his early 40s, extremely devoted to his wife and two daughters. By creating a business built on the concept of exceptional respect for both employees and customers, he had made a significant amount of money. He also was a "recovering drug addict and workaholic," according to his description.

Jerry told me with pride that his recovery was based on his sheer will power, which he had displayed abundantly. I congratulated him for his efforts and explained to him that only 10 percent of recovery from addiction was about arresting the process or abstaining from the substance. The other 90 percent was about waking up or increasing one's awareness and understanding of what deficits we may have experienced in our development.

He was adamant about not wanting to revisit any aspects of his childhood nor to blame his father in order to fix himself. Despite my efforts to assist him in exploring any areas of deprivation within his family in a non-blaming manner, Jerry could not bring himself to revisit his past. We developed an abstinence contract, which he agreed to follow. It included several alternate coping skills to use when he felt the desire or urge to head to the casino.

Jerry followed this contract with great will power for several months and chose to do it alone without the aid of Gamblers Anonymous, myself, or any other people. Then he came to my office one day feeling quite overwhelmed with grief and guilt. He had returned to the casino and missed his daughter's sixteenth birthday. I asked him to tell me what he thought his daughter might have felt about him that day.

He then launched into a series of profane words and derogatory comments about himself that gave me chills, both for their intensity and cruelty. With a little coaching, Jerry was able to describe the numerous times in his own childhood when his father let him down in a similar way. He also began to explore the impact his father's drinking had on him after his mother's death before Jerry's sixth birthday. Most pronounced for Jerry was the deep shame he felt in remembering the filth and poverty he grew up in.

He began to quickly see how he chose to cope by working hard and getting as far away from poverty and his mother as he could all by himself. He was so "all by himself" as a little boy. Jerry was overwhelmed because, despite how hard he had tried to protect his daughters from feeling what he had experienced growing up, he was recreating a similar situation emotionally for them through his gambling addiction.

Jerry was now ready to courageously explore the coping mechanisms he chose as a child and to discard those that no longer worked for him. The most painful one, and the one he least wanted to pass on, was about living "all by himself."

URGES AND PROGRESSION

To understand addiction, it helps to understand the term *overwhelming urge*. Most people can relate this term to the biological sensation of a full bladder. So how can an overwhelming urge be powerful enough to cause people to forget about those they love? Imagine the sense of drowning or the panic created by choking or having a pillow placed over your head as someone tries to slowly suffocate you. Clients have shared these examples with me as they battled their overwhelming urges.

Addiction is progressive. Initially one will seek occasional relief with the process or substance and slowly move on to more regular use. As addiction progresses, so does one's tolerance of its effects. Gradually the addict requires more of the substance or greater stakes at the gambling table to get relief. As tolerance increases so do the addict's defenses and denial system, creating a spiral of despair.

Since we now have a better understanding of the progressive patterns in addiction, we can better assess whether a person is in early, mid, or late stages of the disease. Most people, when they think of addiction, think of the late-stage alcoholic, homeless, jobless person living on the street. This is a misleading stereotype. Very few addicts make it to this stage alive. For most, the last thing they lose is their job as this would challenge their denial too greatly.

Most chemically dependent people are very hard working. You may be surprised to learn that 15 percent are your colleagues, working right along side of you. Their disorder will usually go unrecognized until they get way beyond the mid-phases of addiction. This is partially due to the stereotype and lack of understanding of the progressive nature of addictions. It is also due to our tolerance of some addictions, such as religious addiction, workaholism, and food addiction.

When I mention religious addiction, some people are surprised and ask what this means. I describe it as an overwhelming need to control others with their religious beliefs. Organized religions, political parties, and other groups are not responsible for addiction anymore than Krispy Kreme donuts are responsible for food addiction. However some organizations, by the nature of their rules, doctrines, and dogma appeal more to those already weakened by intolerance, fear, and lack of knowledge. In the absence of humility and self-esteem these traits can be very destructive.

The American Medical Association calls addiction a primary disease, which means it causes other disorders and diseases. An addict will often tell me they drink because they are depressed. Perhaps this is true on one level, but it could also be that their addiction depresses them. I treat addiction before treating other issues, because it is a primary disease. With the addiction arrested, work on marital problems, job dissatisfaction, or other issues becomes more productive. In any case, addicts are unable to recognize the causes of their addiction without accurate yet compassionate descriptions of the effects of their behavior.

Addiction is usually chronic and fatal. The chronic nature of addiction means that, regardless of the years of abstinence or recovery, the addict will be vulnerable to out-of-the-blue urges, usually under stress. They also may reactivate their addiction if they consume the substance again. Of course, in the case of food addiction, one cannot abstain from eating. However one can abstain from eating for emotional comfort.

Far-Reaching Impacts

Those involved with an addict often lose years waiting for a healthy relationship. Sometimes these relationships work out, often they do not. While waiting for the potential goodness in the addict to emerge, they become disappointed as the addict loses most, if not all, of their free will to the addiction. I share the view of Dr. Carl Jung and others who believe many addicts are spiritual seekers with an exceptional desire to know the answer to such philosophical questions as "Why am I on this mudball planet?" Perhaps the intense longing and related restlessness this question produces contributes to the development of the disease.

Addicts magnetically draw people into their world of deception and shame. They can temporarily seduce or charm all but the most suspicious of humans and keep others from holding them accountable for their actions. The young and naive are most vulnerable to seduction by an addict, especially those who find self-worth in doing for others. I find it difficult to watch such seduction. Both participants are usually unaware of the destructive force that underpins their bond yet binds them eventually in a heartless union.

Shari was a petite, intelligent, twenty-one-year-old registered nurse who came into my office at her mother's request. She described herself as confused. Engaged to Rick since her high school graduation, she broke it off within two weeks of meeting Matt. Within six months she was engaged to Matt. Her mother was not impressed with Matt. He smoked marijuana daily, mistreated Shari frequently, and could not hold a job. On the other hand, she described Rick as kind and hard-working. She said he adored Shari.

Shari described Rick as stable but a little boring and predictable. She said Matt was intense and exciting and made her feel alive. She could hear her mother's concerns but defended Matt fiercely. It became clear to me that Shari was involved with a developing addict who needed Shari's drive, financial security, and presence.

In going through Shari's history, the vulnerability to Matt's seduction became apparent. When she was six, her father had left the family, no long able to handle the responsibility of a family. No wonder her mother was so upset. She was watching her daughter recreate her own life. She also described watching Matt manipulate Shari's thoughts, self-worth, and behavior. Was this intentional on his part? Why would Shari trade a stable partner for an addict?

CHAPTER THREE

DEPRIVATION AND PARENTAL FUNCTIONING

DEPRIVATION

As I mentioned in chapter one, deprivation of essential resources in our family (such as security, nurturance, structure, and acceptance) causes us to develop protective defenses and make maladaptive choices in order to cope. Deprivation of resources is most common in families with under-functioning parents or addicted members. It also appears within families facing poverty, mental illnesses, violence, death of a member, or the ongoing disability of a sibling. Overly strict families can produce deprivation of personal acceptance and development. Chaotic and unstructured families can produce security issues. Family resources can be stretched thin with far-ranging results on each member.

THE UNDER-FUNCTIONING PARENT

The greatest impact occurs when the under-functioning member is a parent suffering from addiction or a mental illness such as debilitating depression or severe narcissism. These illnesses generally create the more aggressive survival roles, since they generate greater societal and personal shame. They also produce higher levels of reality distortion due to the manipulative features of these disorders. Consistent and loving grandparents, relatives, and teachers can mitigate the impact of under-functioning parents.

Addiction is responsible for most of the parental under-functioning I see today. Living with an addict is extremely difficult and often called "living in the trenches." The war is over reality. Addicts, whether they are addicted to a substance such as alcohol or a process such as gambling, develop a powerful defense structure. Their defenses include rationalization, minimization, denial, and outright delusion. An addict will throw reality out the window in order to avoid exposure or an interruption of the habit.

My good friend and gifted clinician in the addiction field described finding her questioned "childhood reality" with her Brownie camera. Mary Beth grew up in a family in which most of her relatives were heavy drinkers, especially at family gatherings. She described one very confusing Christmas Day gathering when she was fifteen. Grandma became ill at the dinner table. Mary Beth saw her slump over and began to drool. She called out that something was wrong with Grandma! Her parents and other relatives continued to drink and eat despite her efforts to get their attention. Later that evening, when it was time for the guests to leave, someone mentioned that Grandma needed a ride to the hospital.

Mary Beth learned the next day that her beloved Grandma had had a stroke. She could not come to terms with the unbelievable reality that the family had simply ignored it. So she unconsciously chose to believe she had made it all up rather than accept that something so frightening could happen.

Thirty years later, trying to understand her own alcoholism, Mary Beth decided to dig out the photos she took of her family growing up. Reality came back into focus. She found a little black-and-white photo of the Christmas dinner. In the picture was Grandma slumped over with her face paralyzed and her Dad taking a bite of pecan pie. The story Mary had thought she made up all these years was true. She was not crazy. Thanks to the Brownie camera photo, she finally had proof of her discarded reality.

The Narcissistic or Self-Focused Parent

My training in addictive family dynamics enabled me to see the close parallels in traits and roles created among the children raised by narcissistic parents. Most of us are familiar with the Greek mythological character Narcissus, punished by the gods for rejecting the love of the nymph Echo. His fate was to spend eternity in love with his reflection in a pond, perpetually reaching out for love, only to have it ripple away in every attempt. The gods eventually forgave him and turned him into a beautiful yellow flower.

I have also witnessed either the increase of this population or an increased awareness of the impact of having narcissistic parents, I believe both are happening. It is hard to deny that our literary and media values are influenced by the Me Generation. We dismiss the impact of our relatively young Western nation with its youthful culture emphasizing external values of appearance and status. We are just starting to see an ageing nation seek out more internal identification and self-worth to define itself.

Depending on the severity of the disorder, narcissistic parents tend to see their children as reflections of themselves. They raise their children based on what they need and want versus what their children need. This kind of parenting greatly reduces the chances of children receiving the resources necessary to value themselves. To make matters worse, it is often difficult even in adulthood to recognize one's parent as having been narcissistic. How can one question a parent's devotion when the parent was so fiercely protective of them?

I worked with a successful attorney named Sheila who came to me for codependency counseling after the break up of her second marriage to an alcoholic man. Despite providing codependency counseling for more than twenty-five years, I still struggle with the term. It has become diluted to the point of little meaning. I do not choose to label people as codependent, but rather to assist them in identifying over-functioning patterns or mal-adaptive behaviors destructive to themselves and others within relationships.

Despite Sheila's regular attendance at Al-Anon (a twelve-step support group for friends and family members of alcoholics) for several years, she could not understand the origins of her codependency. She had no history of addiction in her family and both parents functioned at a very high level. She did, however, admit that her mother was very con-trolling and over protective of her. She also cred-ited regular criticism in her childhood as proof of how much her mother loved her and wanted the best for her. Sheila once said, "She even dyed my ugly, red hair black for me in third grade, so I would not stand out so much in my class."

Sheila continued to explore the ways her mother loved her and I simply listened. She began to cou-rageously examine her mother's behaviors from the perspective of a grown woman with her own four-year-old daughter, instead of from the more limited and vulnerable perspective of being that young child. With growing realization, Sheila began to see her mother as being, "just as self-centered as some of my narcissistic clients!"

She also could see what she learned about love from her mother. And when she combined this with her questionable self-worth, she could see how it led her to seek men who could recreate similar feelings. This is both the blessing and the curse of human nature. We tend to repeat the patterns of our primary relationships until we recognize the patterns. Bringing our adult perspective into some of our childhood memories can begin the waking-up process.

How exceptionally compassionate of Sheila never to diminish her love for her mother while examining her behavior. She actually reported feeling more compassion for her mother. She knew from her training and working with narcissistic criminals, that they had experienced injury often equal to or greater than what they had inflicted on others. Understanding does not excuse or pardon destructive behavior. Rather it provides an opening of the heart for forgiveness, so that, eventually, we can forgive and release ourselves from the prison of resentment.

The Over-Functioning Parent

In order to remain in a primary relationship with an addict of any kind, those close to him or her usually need to develop several adaptive behaviors. Unfortunately for most people, the adaptive behaviors they tend to adopt fail to improve the situation.

These well-intentioned but not very constructive behaviors often include over-functioning. By taking over the responsibilities of the under-functioning addict, they inadvertently shield the addict from the consequences of his or her behaviors. Examining these consequences can actually help the addict by removing the defenses that keep them from seeing the effects of their behavior. Remember that most addicts are seeking refuge and relief through their addiction.

Thus a counter-productive relationship results as the over-functioning person seems to take care of the addict. While this provides some short-term satisfaction and self-esteem for the caregiver, it most often leads to the opposite result in the long term. The caregiver often ends up exhausted and emotionally drained. They continue to give, receiving very little, if anything, in return.

Some of my clients find it useful when I describe this situation in terms of an emotional bank account. The caregivers continually make withdrawals to give the addict. But the addict, who is often almost exclusively self-focused, cannot make deposits in return. In the end neither party gets what they need for a sustainable relationship. The addict does not receive the mature, constructive and compassionate support required to make them accountable for their actions. And the non–addict certainly does not enjoy a healthy relationship.

In most instances the under-functioning addict eventually gets wise to the situation, which makes a difficult situation worse. An addict learns that they can depend on the over-functioning caregiver to do more and more for them. They appear to relinquish control to the caregiver who really wants to help. But in reality they continue to refine their ability to indirectly manipulate and control.

It's not hard to imagine the impact on children when one thinks of an over-functioning parent pouring care into an under-functioning addict. The child is deprived of many important things from both parents. These children often become the unintended victims of a tragic dance of over- and under-functioning parents.

The effects of deprivation in the family specific to chemically dependent parents have been widely publicized by many in the field of addiction. I believe Claudia Black, author of *Children of Alcoholics*, summarizes these effects most succinctly by identifying the three rules often unconsciously adopted by children in these families: Don't talk. Don't feel. Don't trust." The child growing up in the shadow of an addict quickly learns not to talk about what is really going on for fear of consequences. They also learn that to feel anything but anger will leave them vulnerable, since they have no one available to support their feelings. Addicts are known for making grandiose commitments they do not follow through on. Over time, their children learn not to trust that people will do what they say they will do.

These three rules are often essential for surviving the harsh emotional atmosphere of an addictive environment. Unfortunately, trusting, talking, and feeling are essential for developing our awareness and identity and for having meaningful relationships. Breaches in trust by a primary caregiver, when experienced at an early age, often cause a child not only to question their ability to trust others but also their ability to trust themselves. The rules do not change just because the child grows and leaves home. To the contrary, adaptation becomes maladaptive and the child continues to survive rather than to live freely.

THE AVERAGE-FUNCTIONING PARENT

The average or near normal functioning parent is often an overlooked group in the fields of psychology, mental health, and addictions. I was trained to focus on and treat pathology. However, the majority of people find themselves in the normal group most of the time. They respond to the ebb and flow of their parental roles and related demands throughout their lives. The average parent focuses on raising a child and developing his or her potential based on the child's desires rather than on the self-esteem needs of the parents.

The average parent may make some mistakes—either over or under functioning—but corrects these errors with humility and respect for themselves and the child. These parents recognize that children require balanced self-care, so they seek guidance in raising their children. They also recognize that children have individual temperaments and may need different kinds of structure and support than their siblings. Most average parents have done some self-examination of their own parents' methods of parenting and have determined which methods may or may not be helpful to their own children. They recognize that their children's needs may be very different from our own in this rapidly changing world.

> You may give them your love but not
> your thoughts.
> For they have their own thoughts.
> You may house their bodies but not
> their souls.
> For their souls dwell in the house of
> Tomorrow, which you cannot visit,
> not even
> in your dreams.
> You may strive to be like them, but seek
> Not to make them like you.
> For life goes not backward nor tarries with
> yesterday.
> —Khalil Gibran, *The Prophet*

CHAPTER FOUR
CHILDHOOD ROLES

SURVIVAL METHODS AND CHILDHOOD ROLES

Children who lack family resources develop survival mechanisms rather than healthy living skills. Virginia Satir developed the concept of role formation in response to childhood stress in her book, *People Making*. She describes these roles as styles of communication. Claudia Black offers a similar view through the eyes of children with alcoholic parents in her book, *It Will Never Happen to Me*. A pioneer in the area of addition, Sharon Wegscheider also addresses survival roles and the impact of addiction on families.

Survival roles help explain the impact of addiction in families. They also help identify patterns people most often develop in response to childhood deprivation and stress. I have observed these roles also within families with ample resources and no significant or prolonged deprivation. However, in such families the children adapt roles only temporarily in response to certain situations and do not maintain them in adulthood.

It has been fascinating, at times, to observe the development of survival roles within organizations and various work settings during times of stress or when a leader becomes impaired or severely under-functioning.

I first learned of childhood survival roles as a framework for understanding alcoholic families when I was completing my college internship in social work. I was surprised to see the same roles in my internship setting. When one of my internship supervisors underwent an intervention for narcotic use during lunch breaks, I realized that I had inadvertently counteracted his under-functioning and growing addictive behaviors by covering for him. My over-functioning was not only counterproductive, it also delayed the supervisor getting much needed help. The role I adopted arose from childhood choices I had made.

Survival Roles Adopted by Children

As children we experience powerful feelings when faced with deprivation in our family. Unfortunately we may not have many coping choices. Though no two children cope exactly the same way, certain patterns prevail. The energy a child spends on developing survival roles cannot be used as it should on developing his or her identity.

The Golden Child Role

Since families suffering deprivation often develop self-worth issues, one or more children may take on the role of achieving worth or success for the family. Generally this is the first-born child, unless he or she rebels and abdicates this role. These children learn fairly young, often by the age of five, that by providing worth to the family, they are loved. They become devoted to achievement in sports or grades or both and tend to be perfectionists. Perfectionism, rather than a character strength, is actually an attempt to cover up the growing shame of the slightest mistake. The fear of being shamed fuels the drive to be perfect and feeds the need to perform even better.

I have yet to meet a human who can perform perfectly. We simply do not have the tools of gods. There is a powerful yet subtle difference between aiming for excellence rather than perfection. I can achieve excellence even on my worst day. I can never reach perfection, even on my best day. There will always be room to do better, which is the glory and the grace of accepting our humanity. Under the curse of living with perfectionism, room to do better represents failure.

The golden child provides the perfect illusion of success for the struggling family. As Greg, one of my clients, stated, "As long as I was heading off to medical school, my family could hide the fact that Mom's depression was killing us kids inside. Nobody talked about her staying in bed for days. Nobody could. Everything looked fine on the outside. Nothing was fine on the inside. I knew if I did not go to med school, Dad would have left us a long time ago."

The golden child (a.k.a. hero) inadvertently becomes a co-conspirator in hiding the family's shame or secret, often at the expense of developing their own identity. They often create a false self-image of a highly independent, super responsible, and disciplined individual. Underneath lives a child terrified of letting others down. The golden child often seeks a partner who needs more than loves them.

By no means are all successful people golden children of deprived families living out a survival role. The key difference lies in the intent of the parents. Did they want him to perform for their worth or his? Does the child feel loved for being or only through doing? In healthy families, children seek success for the internal rewards they bring not for some false, external identity.

Did you seek your own achievements and perform for your own desires and satisfaction or for the needs of your family?

One particular hero's story haunts me to this day for the child's courage. Ron was the oldest child of five. He had four younger sisters and a severely drug-addicted mother, whom his father had left shortly after the birth of his baby sister. Ron's mother was hospitalized and detoxified several times before he was nine. Each time she was taken away, Ron and his sisters were placed in foster care. His sisters hated foster care and his baby sister would often cry out in fear when they headed for separate foster homes. One night, shortly before Ron's tenth birthday, his mother was taken to detox after getting into a bar fight.

When the social worker from the detox unit called to tell Ron to pack for the foster home, he decided to make up a story to protect his baby sister. He said that his aunt had just moved in with them. The social worker was relieved. She had tried without success for months to get a family member to take the children. Ron and his seven-year-old sister, Molly, took turns skipping school to take care of their toddler-age sisters during the day. Ron went to the neighborhood bars in the evening and performed magic tricks in order to get quarters to buy milk, bread, and macaroni for the children to eat. He was too young to cash his mother's food stamps. Ron and his sisters survived this way for several days, sometimes weeks, at a time. His story is a testament to the strength and survival instincts of children.

I met Ron when he was thirty-two and a highly gifted, compassionate counselor. After a bout with alcoholism, he had learned to how to break from his mother's legacy and had let go of his brave, but no longer needed, role as family hero.

THE TROUBLEMAKER OR BLACK SHEEP ROLE

This child provides a needed distraction for the deprived family. The second most common way for a child to cope with stress is to act out or get into trouble. The most likely child to assume this role is the one who already has a trait such as hyperactivity or a learning disability or a strong will. The black sheep unconsciously agrees to carry on the family's shame. The family can look to him or her and say, "If only you would behave, this family would be fine."

In extreme cases the family will actually blame the child for its problems. I have on several occasions had couples bring in their troubled child for help, only to find that the child was acting out to keep the focus off of a failing marriage or a parent's secret. Remember, a child desires, often unconsciously, to keep his or her family intact at all costs to them. This child will often skip school, get in trouble with the law, get pregnant, or find other ways to keep the family's blame on them. They are the most likely to escape their family's shame by using drugs, joining gangs, or running away from home.

Black sheep are obviously disfavored in most class-room settings due to their disruptive behavior. However they are my favorite clients in family counseling sessions. They have the least denial and the most ability to defy the "no talk rule" of many deprived families. They will often say it like it is, but they often do so in a very profane and disrespectful manner. This can undermine their being taken seriously by others and reinforce their belligerent manner. They have little trust in institutions or authority and want to challenge and change the world, at least the world their family created in them. This survival role has captured recent media attention for both its suicidal and homicidal traits when exposed to constant negative reinforcement by peers in the school setting.

THE QUIET CHILD ROLE

A latter-born female with introverted tendencies often assumes the quiet-child role. This child provides relief for the family as she causes no problems what so ever. She keeps to herself and often stays in her room, where she can be found reading and eating. This child has a tendency toward eating disorders as she chooses food over interactions with people for her comfort. Quietly adjusts to most situations, she does not develop full social skills. She appears very independent on the outside and often remains emotionally distant and non-committal in intimate relationships.

The Baby Role

The youngest child usually assumes this role and provides both comic relief and distraction for the family. As the emotional barometer of the family, children in the baby role will do their best to keep the tension level down. They tend to be cute, immature, and often clown around when they feel anxious. They can be rather annoying both in the classroom setting and therapy sessions, as they will do something distracting anytime someone gets close to expressing a real feeling. They are the constant jokesters at work and are often never taken seriously. Due to their fragile, baby-like behavior they are often left out of family secrets and decisions and never quite know what's going on, but they easily feel it. Babies can be the life of the party and quite entertaining at times.

A final note on family roles: All of these roles reflect adaptations to stress and deprivation within the family. Children assume them courageously in order to keep the family functioning. Unfortunately these roles keep us asleep. They protect us from fear and pain, but they also protect us from intimacy and connection with our true nature and that of others.

If the source of deprivation is removed through recovery, remarriage, or other means, this will not undo the family roles. Those affected will continue their behavior until they develop understanding of the purpose of their role and, most important, are taught other ways of expressing feelings and coping with stress.

Family roles are invisibly intertwined with deep roots of loyalty, love, pain, and fear. Therefore, when a member of the family starts to wake up or relinquish a role, there will be significant stress put on the entire root system. It can be demanding for the first member of a family who enters into the process of greater awareness, because their siblings may not be ready to wake up. They may actually be frightened and challenge the individual who starts to speak of the reality of their experiences growing up. Again courage is required. Courage that is guided by a child is poignant, but can lead to compulsive avoidance of fear. Courage that is guided by awareness will lead to freedom and perhaps, enlightenment.

SECTION TWO
WAKING UP

> The millions are awake enough for physical labor; but only one in a million is awake enough for effective intellectual exertion, only one in a hundred million to a poetic or divine life. To be awake is to be alive. I have never yet met a man who was quite awake. How could I have looked him in the face?
> —Henry David Thoreau, *Walden*

What does it mean to be awake or aware? I often use the metaphor of a play when I attempt to understand or explain this concept. I can view myself as the actor on a stage, unconscious except for knowing my next line, and with minimal responsibility for the outcome. Or I can view myself as the producer and director of my life, choosing the actors, choosing all the other elements of the production with a conscious understanding of their impact on one another and always assuming responsibility for the results, though they may not have been intended or predicted.

I remember being very saddened in a graduate psychology class, when I learned of the classic duck experiment. In the design, baby ducks were assigned either a real mother duck or a robotic imitation. While the robotic duck could feed and teach the new ducklings, it was programmed to inflict painful bites periodically. Over time the ducklings with the robotic mother were unable to separate or increase their distance from it. The ducklings assigned to the real mother were able to move farther and farther from her each day, eventually going off on their own. The ducklings in the robotic group stayed with their "mother" till they died.

I could not help but think of the blind loyalty I had witnessed working with people who were either raised in non-nurturing families or in abusive relationships. Just as the baby ducks waited their lifetime to receive what they needed, so often humans do the same.

> Most contemporary therapists who work in depth with their patients know that behind the rigid top heavy posture of most contemporary men is a little child with years of stored up tears and fears.
> —Stephen Larson

If we create a role in childhood and do not examine its nature as we grow older, we may feel like we are still children pretending or acting as grown ups. We will seek out others to parent us, direct us, or write a part to play in their life. If we chose a pseudo-independent role, we will seek others to direct and perform for us. It can be overwhelming to begin to wake up and realize we are becoming as narcissistic as a parent may have been. Or to wake up to the fact that our selfless nature actually exploits others.

Hurtful behavior does not necessarily reflect our intent but rather our unmet normal dependency needs. Remember the basic requirements all children need in order to grow up—acceptance, security, nurturance, structure, and emotional support consistently shown over time. It was our parents' responsibility to fulfill these needs in our childhood. If they were unable to do so, it becomes our task as we grow up.

> A mother such as we once urgently needed—empathic and open, understanding and understandable, available and usable, transparent, clear, without unintelligible contradictions—such a mother was never ours, indeed she could not exist; for every mother carries with her a bit of her 'unmastered past,' which she unconsciously hands on to her child. Each mother can only react empathically to the extent that she has become free of her own childhood, and she is forced to react without empathy to the extent that, by denying the vicissitudes of her early life, she wears invisible chains.
> —Alice Miller, *The Drama of the Gifted Child*

CHAPTER FIVE
PATTERNS IN RELATIONSHIPS

Sometimes we avoid waking up by holding our parents responsible for the task. This is usually not evident on a conscious level, but can be picked up by examining how old we feel inside when interacting with them. It becomes easier for me to recognize unresolved needs I have when I feel like a sixteen year-old around my father.

Ask yourself if there are any patterns in your relationship with your parents that are uncomfortable for you? What purpose did they serve?

I worked with a woman who was talented and beautiful inside and out. However Anita was dying from anorexia. She had several in-patient hospital treatments over the course of her thirty years but always relapsed within a few weeks. As she became more responsible in her own self-assessment, she began to notice resentments and regressive tendencies whenever she interacted with her father. She found this confusing, because she adored her father and understood his alcoholism, having spent years in Alateen, a twelve-step program for teenagers and young adults. I asked her to simply sit with her feelings for a few minutes after her next visit with her father and explore what she wanted most from him.

She quickly heard a voice screaming in her mind, "I am not going to eat until you stop drinking!" She recognized this voice as that of herself at thirteen and remembered making a secret pact with her father. If he was going to choose to drink and die then she was going with him. She had the intellectual skills to recover, but she lacked the awareness of an emotional decision she had made at thirteen.

Our intellect may forget such a powerful decision, but not by our emotions. Once Anita recognized her decision, she was able to reevaluate it from an adult perspective versus that of a scared and lonely thirteen-year-old child. This is not to say that changing her decision didn't require courage. She had to surrender not only her illusions of control and her magical thinking but also her misguided loyalty toward her father. Anita chose to live whether her father found recovery or not. She also chose to eat in a healthy manner and two years later had a successful pregnancy. She named the baby after her father.

Some call the behavior of "sitting with your feelings" reflection; some call it self-examination. Whatever it's called, it is an essential tool for waking up. Sometimes simply being is more important than doing in the waking process.

The relationship patterns we develop with our spouses or partners can be very revealing about ourselves. We often recreate in our marriage the very dynamics we used to address our childhood dependency or deprivation. Unfortunately, instead of seeing our own patterns, we often focus on our mate's corresponding or compensating patterns. Many people miss real opportunities to resolve their hurtful relationship patterns by leaving or divorcing or vilifying their spouse. A divorce or separation may very well be indicated. However, unless separating partners take the time to achieve some level of awareness of their roles in the relationship, they are likely to set up similar or corresponding opposite dynamics in their next relationship.

> Your failures will be helpful. They can show you how unconscious you are. And even if you can become aware that you are unconscious, you have gained certain awareness. If a madman becomes aware that he is mad, he is on the path toward sanity.
> —Osho, *Awareness*

It can be difficult to recognize parental narcissistic injuries until they create havoc in our relationships. Narcissistic injury is basically the result of parental neglect of our emotional needs. Parents do not set out to neglect their children but may fail to recognize emotional needs as legitimate, especially if the parent failed to have similar needs met.

Most of us came into this world screaming out for someone to meet our needs. This is healthy narcissism and essential for survival. As our needs get met, they dissolve. This requires parents who understand what we truly need to thrive as opposed to what we want. This kind of parental love that withstands all demands without giving in, endures the battles over "but I really need that," and stays awake in the middle of the night sometimes to ponder the needs and desires of their child.

The most basic emotional need we have is to be loved for who we are and not for the qualities or traits esteemed by our parents. Some narcissistic parents may pamper and indulge a child for the enhanced self-esteem they enjoy, not out of love for the child or recognition of what the child needs. Other narcissistic injury comes from parental lack of empathy or from placing their desires above our legitimate needs. A minor form of this is telling our children not to cry when it is inconvenient for us to attend to them. A major form is indirectly telling our child what they should be when they grow up in order to make us proud.

We can defend ourselves from overtly narcissistic parental demands far better than less obvious ones. Did your parents display any demands on you that were driven by narcissism?

Intellectual abilities in children rarely come under attack from narcissistic parents or siblings. Therefore, the hallmark of narcissistic injury usually involves a heavy emphasis on intellectual achievement. In knowing this, a question to ask yourself would be, "Is my knowledge safe to share with others, but not my feelings?"

Things do not change, we do.
—Henry David Thoreau

If you recognized or took on the traits of any specific role identified in Section One due to a deprived family, the most likely pattern you will struggle with in relationships is maintaining self-care. Since taking care of the self may have felt or been labeled selfish in a deprived family, healthy self-care may actually feel self-centered. This is especially true if the source of deprivation was a sibling's or parent's chronic illness or death.

Katie, a friend of mine, was fifteen when her brother was in a car accident that left him severely brain damaged. The accident was hard on Katie's family, but they bravely chose to care for her brother in their home instead of a nursing home. She was a healthy, strong willed, somewhat defiant adolescent before the accident. After the accident, she stopped testing her parents' limits and dedicated her strong will to helping them cope. She appeared to fully recover from the toll of the accident when she was able to separate from her parents and head to college.

It was not until she had her second child, a strong-willed boy, that she began to experience the symptoms of her choice to shut down her will and her adolescent development. She began to yell at and judge her son as selfish whenever he tested her limits or displayed his defiance. Despite knowing that this was normal and healthy for a thirteen-year-old child, she could not stop her over-reactions. It was not until she spoke of her struggles with her old high school friends that she connected her choice at fifteen to her over-reaction to her son's behavior. It reminded her of the day she skipped school to protest the war, which reintroduced her to the spirited person she was at her son's age. She recalled how much her parents loved her rebellious spirit and was finally able to grieve for the part of her she had buried long ago. Her empathy for her son returned as she relearned how to accept herself.

THE GOLDEN CHILD PATTERNS

The golden child often develops his or her identity and self-esteem around taking care of people and chalking up achievements. They will often seek out injured people to heal and choose an under-functioning partner. This explains the appeal of a bad boy or bad girl. The golden child argues, "They simply need to be loved and tamed." Not true, we need to fix them in order to continue to feed our self-worth. If you have these tendencies, it is important that you validate your worth by who you are and not by whom you are saving.

By submerging their intimacy needs under their need to perform, golden children can sometimes become workaholics. Workaholism can be recognized far more easily in the office, but is just as prevalent in the home. Domestic workaholics are perpetually on the move cleaning, cooking, and taking care of people. The behavior itself is not the problem. Rather, the problem is the need to gain self-worth by doing more, which can never be fully attained this way.

There will always be more to do. The workaholic never achieves the gratification we attain when healthy self-love fuels our work. The first step toward awareness for these individuals is to suffer through the feelings created by doing nothing and simply being for several minutes each day until intimacy or a connection with the self is found.

The Troublemaker or Black Sheep Pattern

The troublemaker usually has anger issues, which create havoc in relationships. Troublemakers can be explosive or sullen when they express their feelings. They need to learn to talk out instead of acting out their powerful feelings. Without awareness of their role in the family, they may unintentionally set themselves up to be victimized in relationships. They may benefit by recognizing that their offensive behavior affects how they are treated. It can be hard for them to give up the victim stance because it entails taking on responsibility for their actions. I take a rather hard stance with anyone after the age of eighteen (other than those in physically abusive relationships) who tells me they have little choice in their relationship patterns. There are few true victims in adult relationships. We have the choice to leave or protect ourselves whether we see it or not.

Troublemakers may struggle with setting limits internally for they tend to struggle equally with commitment and fidelity in their primary relationship. They often project their struggle onto their partner with concerns over his or her loyalty. Of all the roles, the troublemaker has the most issues with trusting people. They need to develop awareness of their decision to mistrust people and to experience the feelings that necessitated that decision.

The Quiet Child Patterns

An important reminder here is that there are degrees to which we develop survival roles. Many people have some quiet-child characteristics and tend to avoid stress and other people at times. The key question is whether they do so out of awareness and choice or out of fear and unconscious decisions made a long time ago.

The quiet child is the least likely to marry. They seek comfort in solitude versus interacting with people. They avoided people and situations in their childhood as their primary way of coping. Awareness, or allowing the feeling of loneliness to surface and be expressed, is the first step in waking up for these individuals. They tend to be reclusive and prefer their own company over the risk of chaotic human interaction. They may feel inept in social settings but can fairly easily be taught social skills. Waking up for them often involves addressing compulsive behaviors they may have developed, such as food addiction, hoarding items, TV or video addiction, and, pornography addiction.

The Baby Patterns

The baby or clown is generally lots of fun in a relationship because they know how to play. A clown will act out with humor rather than express intimate needs. This behavior can block meaningful relationships. For example, if people don't take you seriously, you may want to examine how you reinforce their behavior. Clowns tend to clown around, which can be troublesome in romantic relationships, except with another clown. Immature or baby-like behavior can be a mechanism for avoiding emotional intimacy.

It is important to identify the traits in ourselves as well as to the original vulnerabilities being activated in our relationships. People married to alcoholics, need to understand their need to seek out an under-functioning partner or impaired partner. If they were seduced or manipulated into a relationship, they may have unmet needs that create gaps in their judgment.

Just as water seeks its own level, we seek people with similar levels of maturation, self-esteem, narcissism, and shame. Issues we identify in our partners may be issues we need to address. On the other hand, we may actually have opposite issues, but they usually will correspond. Because we are meant to evolve, we seek out those who have issues we need to resolve through greater awareness.

CHAPTER SIX

HUMILITY

A human looks up to the universe and
exclaims,
"I exist!"
The Universe responds back,
"That fact, however, does not create in
me any sense of obligation."
—Anonymous

How We Loose Humility

In most Western religions or Eastern practices, humility is a requirement for spiritual growth. Without humility we will not seek greater awareness nor will we wake up. The paradox that many struggle with is that they do not have the self-esteem to admit their human limitations or what I call divine imperfections. Surrendering to our humanity is the path back to waking up. Some religions call this accepting grace. Some therapists have called it unconditional love. I like to call it compassion for the self.

Very few people I interact with have much self-compassion. It takes solid defenses to protect ourselves from the constant, cold judgments we make about ourselves. The more we injure ourselves through negative self-talk or perfectionist tendencies, the greater our defenses become.

The process of loosing humility often starts innocently in a child who has not been given a sense of worth or value. The first big lie we tell others, out of fear of being bad and punished, begins the process. We lay the first building block in our defense structure when we start to believe the lie. Then we start to minimize our negative behaviors instead of taking responsibility for them. Gradually we learn that blaming others also protects our fragile self-worth. If we do not have empathic, emotionally responsive caretakers we may need even greater defenses to protect ourselves. This is where arrogance, false pride, grandiosity, and narcissism eventually take over to insulate us from our growing self-hatred. These defenses gradually put us asleep to our true selves, to our humility, and, eventually, to our ability to feel empathy. Waking up involves the process of surrendering our defenses by admitting and eventually accepting our humanness.

The First Step

The first step in most twelve-step programs reads as follows, "We admitted we were powerless over (fill in the blank with your compulsive or destructive behavior) and that our lives have become unmanageable."

These words succinctly describe the process of trading in our false pride and defenses for interdependence and humility. Step one contains multiple coping skills, if one takes the time to sit with it.

The first word, we, is not there by accident. We human beings have been designed to be interdependent and mutually supporting. In accepting the we nature of our human design, we accept our healthy need for other people. We do not loose this trust in a vacuum. We loose it when we are let down or bruised in a relationship. Our patterns of interacting with others began in relationships. Therefore, our roles or patterns need to be both recognized and felt within relationships. We cannot wake up without humbly accepting our need for others to help us. Often this help means simply listening or witnessing another person's story.

Many of us have made it our life's work to be independent. Independence is fine for many tasks, but awareness requires interdependence. *Counterdependent* is actually the word to describe those who deny their healthy dependency needs. They may state as their creed as, "I do not need anybody!" Again, paradoxically, counter-dependent people generally have the highest unmet dependency needs and the most fear of acknowledging them to themselves or others.

The second word in this step is *admitted*, which is actually the entrance word for the process of acceptance. We are admitting to ourselves that we are fully human. We may admit that we have addictions or we may admit to patterns that don't work. We may even admit that we do not like ourselves very much.

The next major word is *powerless*. This word causes confusion and concern for many I have worked with. When I admit my powerlessness over a behavior, I then have more responsibility to address it, not less, as some believe. Once I recognize and admit any problem, I then have greater choice and greater liability. The nature of powerlessness thus drives me to seek other resources for assistance. It does not, in any manner, reduce my responsibility to address my powerlessness. It simply implies that I need other resources besides myself to arrest or change the behavior. This is the case in addiction as well as with any other issue, disease, or pattern which one cannot resolve on one's own.

When my children were sick and I would admit my powerlessness or limitations in relieving their illness. This did not release me from being responsible for them and seeking medical care. Rather it further compelled me to take action.

The first step can also be very helpful in identifying that which we do and do not have power over. I am constantly amazed at how much energy and anxiety people exert over trying to control what they have absolutely no power over. In recognizing that I cannot control most things, I become free to use my energy to focus on what I can control.

I often hear the following analogy of powerlessness. I have total control over my garden and what I plant and grow and how much weeding I do. I do not have control over the weather or the rain. I also have little, if any, control over my neighbor's garden. I do like to go over and tell my neighbor what she should plant, but I am powerless if she chooses not to listen. I could, in fact, spend so much time watching my neighbor and his weeds grow, that I forget about my own garden. How much time do you invest in trying to change others versus pulling your own weeds?

The final word in this step, *unmanageable*, addresses the consequences of our sleepy behavior. By viewing the specific consequences of ignoring my powerlessness and its related effects on my self and others, I can diminish the impact of my defense system. If I have fewer defenses insulating me from reality, I can then feel the need to take action.

An example is taken from my own struggle with nicotine addiction. I can defend the fact that I may die twenty years sooner with either, "I will take my chances" or "I do not want to outlive my children." I am a skilled at minimizing the risk. When I took some time and wrote out the specific consequences I was experiencing from my smoking,—such as loss of smell and taste, loss of self-respect, and loss of

free will—it was impossible to minimize the consequences or the feelings I really had about smoking.
I soon went on to give up my nicotine for freedom,
but not without help and a plan that addressed
the factors of why I smoked.

Understanding specifically and clearly that I was
poisoning myself with tobacco was the beginning
of my first step. Understanding the reasons or the
purpose of this self-inflicted poisoning was essential
for taking the next step.

To summarize this key step: By admitting and humbly surrendering to our powerlessness, we energize
ourselves to take responsible action. By understanding the consequences or unmanageable aspects
of our previous behavior, we are less likely to fall
back asleep into our defenses.

> If the Angel designs to come it will be
> because you have convinced her, not
> by tears but your humble resolve to be
> always beginning: to be a beginner.
> —Rainer Maria Rilke

How We Get it Back

The process of admitting our divine imperfections
leads us into a state of humility. I have often found
that my character defects are actually protecting
my character strengths until they feel safe enough

to come out of hiding. My self-centered behavior protects my selfless nature until I have the strength to navigate in this world without protection. The more I admit my human imperfections, the more glimpses I have into my divine nature.

I hear many people today report that they believe they are spiritual beings attempting to live in a human world. This may well be the case. However, I have observed that these divine or spiritual characteristics require a strong human self-worth in order to emerge. As I mentioned earlier, if we try to lead with our spiritual traits before accepting and understanding our human nature, we will be taking a shortcut. This detour can lead to co-dependent and enabling behavior or worse—a life of being used by others. Paradoxically, surrendering to our humility brings strength of character. What character strengths are you hiding under your human imperfections?

CHAPTER SEVEN
BOUNDARY AND IDENTITY DEVELOPMENT

DEFENSES OVER DEVELOPMENT

As children we choose naturally to focus our energy on developing a sense of self. We want to learn both how we work and how the world works. When our energy needs to be directed toward feeling safe or helping our family function, we will not fully develop a sense of self. We will need to develop defenses to protect us instead of healthy boundaries that define us. Many of the defenses we choose enable us to survive. However they also enable others to under-function.

I have a rather direct definition of enabling behavior. It is any behavior that helps to preserve and protect pathology. As loving children why would we do such a thing? Out of love, we decide to sacrifice our needs for the needs of our parents. If a parent is emotionally needy, we may achieve very little emotional growth. We will, however, get ample training in enabling others to under-function. Doing for others what they should be doing for themselves is another definition of enabling. As a child, though, how can I be expected to tell Mom or Dad not to come to me for their emotional needs? As a child,

I do not even know what my emotional needs are yet. Did you believe one of your parents needed you to be there for them?

There are degrees of enabling behavior. One of the most severe forms happens when we help protect a parent's addiction or hide their abusive behavior. The child's world is his family and he will bravely do anything to keep the family together, even if it means covering for his parent. We don't automatically stop this behavior once we leave home and reach adulthood. We will most likely continue to enable people at work and even our own children. However by protecting others from the consequences of their behavior, we allow their pathology, or addiction, or under-functioning to continue.

Sue grew up under an emotionally distant mother but managed to do well in college and start a life of her own. She married a research scientist who liked to smoke marijuana. Since she and her siblings had smoked marijuana in high school, she did not see it as particularly harmful and thought her intelligent husband would outgrow it. As his smoking increased, she became more concerned. One afternoon the landlord came over to fix the broken water heater. As he was leaving, he spotted tall plants lining the back of the house. He immediately recognized them as marijuana and asked what they were doing on his property. Before Sue could even think, she said, "My husband is conducting an important research project on the medicinal value of marijuana. He has a license to grow it." The landlord knew her husband had published similar research on plants, so accepted her answer and left.

Sue was in shock by her quick ability to lie and sought help for herself. It did not take Sue long to realize that she had mastered her ability to lie before the age of ten. Her mother had often warned her to not tell her father that she had spent most of the day in bed with depression. Sue also knew that if her father found out about her mother, she would be sent away again to that "icky green hospital." For the first time, Sue began to see how her innocent, childhood behavior kept her mother from getting the help she needed. She also realized that to lie and protect her husband would prevent him from getting help. With a little practice and support, Sue was able to resign as her husband's enabler and set boundaries. She told him she would need to leave and live elsewhere if he did not destroy his marijuana plants and seek help. He honored her boundaries that afternoon and began treatment for marijuana addiction three days later.

A less dramatic form of enabling occurs when we do for our children what they need to do for themselves. It is appropriate and nurturing to help tie my four-year-old child's shoes. (I love Velcro.) It is not nurturing to tie my eight-year-child's shoes because she is whining and tired. Sometimes we enable our children simply because it is easier. In the long run, it may not be easier. There are very few shortcuts that work in parenting.

To increase our awareness of any enabling behavior patterns we may have, it is helpful to ask ourselves some questions. Whose responsibility is this? Am I the one responsible for calling the boss if my husband is too hung over to work? Should I be the one to finish my child's homework? Is it my fault if my father does not love my mother? The more adult responsibilities we had as children, the more we may feel responsible for nearly everyone and everything going on around us. We have responsibilities *to* other people, such as our spouses and children. We are not responsible *for* them.

When we feel responsible for others, we expect them to live up to our expectations so we can feel OK. This can require quite a bit of manipulation. When we are responsible to others, we have much more empathy for them and much less fear of them failing us.

Is this behavior really helping? The more unbalanced reinforcement we received as children for being a good helper, the more our worth may be dependent on helping others at all costs. This is not to say that praise for a child's industriousness is negative. It just needs to be balanced with praise for their inherent worth. Covering regularly for your inept co-worker may not be really helping him or others. Giving your child a ride to school every day instead of allowing her to take the bus (as long as the bus is safe), may not be teaching her a useful value. Giving money to an addict is very seldom helpful.

What are my motives or intent? As children we may have enabled our parents in order to keep peace or survive or both. We also can enable out of guilt. If I missed my son's choir concert due to work, he knows I am an easy mark for several days. Many parents going through divorce report tremendous feelings of guilt regarding their children and temporarily back off on limit setting out of guilt. This creates havoc on the children as they call for the consistency of ongoing structure and limits during this transition. To be sure, children will really test limits at this time, just like I test the lock on my door after a neighborhood burglary.

Parents who have suffered deprivation often try to overcompensate through their children. The most dramatic example of this is seen in the parent who was abused as a child. Less than 30 percent of these parents go on to physically abuse their children. A majority go on to be afraid of setting limits and do not provide enough structure and discipline for their children.

One last word about intent, only you truly know your intent. I get saddened when people take a rigid view of enabling without compassionate understanding. At Al-Anon one evening I heard a woman describe her financial struggles. She was taking over the household bills for her alcoholic husband. Other members reminded her that this was enabling behavior and it would stop her husband from getting the help he needed. Yes, it may have been enabling. However, her primary intent was to keep the lights and heat on for her young children.

These questions can be helpful in waking ourselves up to enabling behavior patterns, but in order to stay awake, we need to replace enabling with effective skills. Boundary setting is one of the most effective skills in managing relationships. In an ideal family, boundary development goes hand in hand with identity development and growth. Healthy boundaries assist us in both defining and maintaining our identity. They simply create borders around our sense of self. Boundaries not to be confused with walls or defenses, which serve to protect us from reality.

VISUALIZATION OF BOUNDARIES

To understand your own boundaries, you may want to try this visualization exercise. It is best to first read through the exercise, then close your eyes and create the fort, remembering as much detail as you wish.

In your mind create a perfect fort for yourself. You are free to place this fort in any setting you choose.

What would the fort look like? What are the walls made out of? How do you light your fort? How would you furnish it? What items for comfort would you bring into the fort? Would people visit it? How would they enter? Do you feel safe in it? Why or why not? Take a few moments to just sit in your fort.

After completing this exercise, take some time to think of your fort as metaphor for your boundaries. Do you admit people easily? Are there any people you would not want in your fort? Are the walls well defined? Do you feel basically safe? Why or why not? By answering some of these questions, you get a better idea of the concept of boundaries and how they may apply to you.

Defining our boundaries helps us define ourselves. Setting boundaries helps us maintain ourselves in a respectful and loving manner. In defining our boundaries it can be helpful to begin by asking how well you define the difference between another person's feelings and your own. Do you get angry when another person is angry? Feelings are not contagious unless we have insufficient boundaries. Empathy for another is not the same as feeling their feelings for them.

If our parents are not aware of the importance of emotional boundaries, they may not be able to teach us how to tell the difference between some-one else's feelings and our own. Some parents may be so needy themselves that they expect their children to carry their feelings for them. An example of this is when a parent is angry with their spouse and vents this anger onto the child. Another example is when a parent does not take responsibility for managing their feelings appropriately in front of a child. Parents do not need to be stoic in front of their children, but rather teach them how to manage feelings. If a child is around a fearful and anxious parent, the child will inadvertently absorb the anxiety. Since children are just forming their boundaries and are highly permeable, like little emotional sponges.

I remember one of my first lessons in emotional boundaries. At the age of five, I found my mother in the hallway crying on the phone. I had never seen her cry before. She was nine months pregnant with my brother. I began to cry with her. She caught me out of the corner of her eye and put the phone down. Despite her labor pains, she told me she was crying because she was going to have a baby very soon. She said I did not need to cry for her and that it was normal for women to cry when the baby was coming. I stopped crying and asked her why? At that moment my father came in, grabbed her arm, and led her directly across the street to the hospital where my brother was almost born in the elevator.

Years later, when my son was about to be born in the hospital entrance, I fully understood the answer to my question. More importantly, my mother had taken the time to teach me an important lesson in emotional boundaries.

How do I know if I need to set a boundary? The most common "red oil light" indicators for needing a boundary are feelings of rage or anger and the behaviors of whining or complaining. Other common feelings that alert us to insufficient boundaries are feeling like a victim or feeling threatened by another person's words or behavior. Our struggle usually isn't with what others are doing to us, but rather what we allow done to us. We teach others how to treat us by what we allow and do not allow in our relationships.

If I am raised in a family that welcomed my independence and growing boundary development, I will be less afraid to set boundaries. Many people I work with are not only afraid to set boundaries and limits with others; they do not believe they have the right to do so! In some families, boundaries may not be encouraged at all, especially if the child was raised with a no-talk rule, because of familial shame. Breaking this rule and stating what you need may be very scary for some. If this is the case for you, expect to feel uncomfortable and afraid when setting limits the first few times. If you were taught that it is selfish to ask for what you need, you may feel ashamed of setting boundaries. If this is the case, you may want to compassionately reflect on the times you actually were being selfish.

It may have appeared selfish to my dear friend Jane's father, when he found her in conflict over her curfew with her mother. However, it was normal for Jane, since she was sixteen and did not know that her mother was about to loose her job. Would it have been selfish even if Jane had known about her mother's stress?

Assertive and respectful communication, instead of avoidant behavior, helps us set and maintain boundaries. The best are set with clear limits, a calm voice, and in as few words as possible. Some examples: "No, I will not do that." "Yes, I will do that." If you use anger to set boundaries, most people, especially children, will know it may be removed as soon as your anger has been vented. Anger is a hot, quick-burning fuel, which does not support strong boundary setting.

Respect for others is important in setting our boundaries. However, respect does not include taking care of another person's feelings. Sometimes respecting ourselves with boundaries is scary or hurtful to others. This is especially true if we set a boundary to leave a harmful relationship, if destructive behavior continues. If we have been over-functioning in our role at work or as a parent or spouse, it is natural for others to react when we resign from doing their tasks. The most common reactions will home in on any unresolved guilt or inadequacy feelings you may have.

You must sometimes do the thing you think you cannot do.
—Eleanor Roosevelt

Sara had been taking care of people since she was seven. Her mother had to work two shifts each day due to her father's paralysis and high medical needs. She fed, bathed, and tucked in her three younger sisters each night after school and did so till she was nineteen. Sara promised herself she would never be in her mother's position. She then went on to graduate from medical school with honors.

Amazingly all the children in this family went on to be attorneys or physicians. They could have just as easily chosen drugs or maladaptive relationships. Sara married in her thirties and, after a difficult pregnancy, had a beautiful baby girl named Nora. When Sara came to my office she was exhausted and being treated for both depression and severe migraines. She strongly believed both her disorders were related to stress and wanted stress reduction tools. After she described her day, I needed a yoga class. She was up at five a.m. to get Nora and herself ready for the day, which included dropping the baby off at day care before work at a small rural family practice clinic.

She then would pick the baby up after work, stop for groceries, come home, and cook dinner for her family of three. After dinner her husband would go to the garage to "putter," while she got the baby bathed and ready for bed. She then would clean the house and start the laundry. At ten p.m. she usually read current medical journals for an hour or two. Guess what my first question was? No, her husband did not work at home, but did do "hobbies and woodworking" in his garage. I asked why he did not work. She stated, "He decided to give up his nursing career after the baby was born to stay home with her, but this turned out to be too stressful for him. He just could not take care of an infant."

Sara defended her husband when she saw my concerned look, stating, "He makes beautiful toys and furniture for Nora during the day. Then he is tired in the evening and just needs to go to the garage and unwind." I asked Sara why she did not expect her husband to help. She said she never thought of asking him for any help. The fact that he was not lying in bed draining the family funds was all the help Sara expected from a husband. Her siblings had all chosen not to marry due to their poor choices in relationships, so Sara did not have any close models of functional spouses.

We began her stress reduction with a boot-camp version of boundary setting exercises. I was very concerned that her apathy for her own life might hinder her ability to set boundaries. I asked her how she felt about her daughter growing up with a father nearly as absent as her own father. Sara let the question sink in below her defenses and beyond her walls, then started to wake up with feelings of grief and anger.

Often people have more compassion and protective instincts for their children than for themselves. This can be useful in finding the energy and courage to set boundaries. We believe that the issues and boundaries we fail to address will get passed on in one form or another to our children. Sara began by setting household responsibility boundaries, dividing them in two. Her husband initially protested and complained that her depression medication was not working (her most vulnerable area). When Sara did not give in to her guilt and maintained her boundary of equal household responsibility, he told her he was depressed. She told him she expected him to take good care of himself and get to a physician for help as soon as possible.

This was so hard for Sara! It felt to her like she was asking her paralyzed father to walk, but she was invested in making sure her daughter had a chance to have a functional father. Sara's husband turned out to be very depressed and responded quite well to treatment. He eventually did go back to work and grew in his ability to interact with his daughter. Sara continued to wake up and shared her enlightenment with her siblings. She even convinced one of them to consider dating one of her totally functional co-workers. Sara's migraines were coming only monthly when she terminated stress-reduction counseling.

Be prepared to enforce and back up your boundaries! As Sara's story illustrates, your boundaries will be tested. Have a back up plan for when they are challenged. It is helpful to never set a boundary you cannot keep. If you are not willing to leave a marriage, do not threaten to divorce your spouse if he or she does not stop an annoying behavior. If you are not ready to watch your child live on the street, do not tell him he must stop using drugs or move out. Until you are willing to look for another job, do not tell your boss to do his own Christmas shopping.

BED BOUNDARIES

The teen mom population provides a distressing and heart-rending example of lack of boundary identity and setting. I have worked with "children" in their second pregnancy before the age of seventeen. These teens often came from homes where sexuality was a no-talk subject, so they explored this area on their own without the protection of defined values or boundaries. I employ an acronym for boundaries with this adventurous group. I call it the BED boundary. I ask them to agree to not engage in further sexual activity until they set the BED boundary with their partner.

This BED boundary includes discussing and deciding on prevention of more Babies and the Emotional meaning and commitment level of the sexual encounter. Most teen girls believe making love means that they are loved. Sometimes their partner is not of the same emotional mind and sees sex as a form of recreation. Understanding a partner's values before going to bed with can prevent heartache. It can also decrease romantic delusions common to most teens. The final and most important aspect of the bed boundary is preventing Diseases. It is important for all people to understand that any sexual encounter exposes one to a host of life-changing diseases.

By no way does the BED boundary attempt to be moral or spiritual. It is a simple tool to help young people learn how to protect themselves emotionally, physically, and socially until they develop sufficient identity and awareness to make healthy choices on their own.

I am surprised at times by the number of so-called adults who have not yet developed their sexual boundaries and find the BED boundary useful. It is ironic to me that these same adults would not think of eating food that was spoiled or drinking the water in a neighboring country. Yet the chance they take with their sexuality exposes them to far more harmful consequences. Many people are asleep sexually, often due to their seeking love in dangerous places.

The following is a Sufi story that illustrates this point. Sufi stories are metaphorical and meant to be read three times, once for entertainment, then for self-application, and finally for wakefulness.

> Searching in the Wrong Place
> Late one evening a neighbor found Nas-ruddin on his hands and knees under the only streetlamp in the village square.
> "What are you searching for, Mullah?"
> "My key."
> Both men got on their knees to search. After a while the neighbor said, "Where precisely did you loose it?"
> "At home in my kitchen."
> "Good Lord! Then why are you searching for it here under the street lamp?"
> "Because it's brighter here."
> —Anthony de Mello, *The Song of the Bird*

Once you start developing boundaries, you will quickly see new aspects of your identity start to emerge. These aspects are parts of you that went into hiding a long time ago. It's as if a part of your being shouts, "It's safe to come out now. Someone is finally watching out for me."

This leads us to the next phase of waking up, which involves reclaiming or developing the aspects of our identity or soul. In different cultures, identity or soul loss was considered to be the highest form of affliction. The men of medicine, called Shamans, were brought in to help in retrieving the aspects of a person that might have been frightened away or captured by someone's cruelty. Some Western religions maintain a separation between the soul and the identity and support giving up the self in exchange for spiritual development. This is not helpful to those who have not begun to develop the self.

How can we give up something we have yet to know? The simplicity of interpretation for some religious doctrines maintains an abundant supply of clients for our counseling practices.

CHAPTER EIGHT
SHAME AND SELF IDENTITY

Our worst fear is not that we are inadequate; our deepest fear is that we are powerful beyond measure. It is our light, not our darkness that most frightens us. We ask ourselves, "Who am I to be brilliant, gorgeous, talented and fabulous?" Actually, who are you not to be? There is nothing enlightened about shrinking so that other people won't feel insecure around you. As we are liberated from our own fear, our presence automatically liberates others.
—Nelson Mandela in *A Return to Love*, by Marianne Williamson

FEELING WICKED

The sense of shame plays a powerful role in stopping our identity development. In order to live with this feeling, we usually need to put ourselves in a deep sleep of unawareness. Many confuse the toxic nature of shame with the invigorating feeling of guilt. It is helpful to separate these two feelings in order to better understand their roles in shaping who we are.

Guilt feelings tell me that my behavior has violated of my values and identity. In other words guilt acknowledges, "I made a mistake." The energizing aspect of guilt helps us find a way to make amends. With guilt there is usually a sense of being able to fix it. Guilt keeps us in line with our principles and helps us to know ourselves.

Shame, on the other hand, attacks the core of our soul and challenges our right to exist. Shame is not about feeling bad for your behavior. It creates a sense of feeling bad about who you are. This is how the wicked or bad child image is created. When we feel shame, we feel hopeless and inadequate at being able to make amends. Some go so far as feeling self-destructive or suicidal. Shame destroys our sense of innocence and blocks the concept of experiencing grace. Shame is not energizing, but rather paralyzing, in its intensity.

So by understanding the difference between shame and guilt, we can move on to explore how we may give or receive shame. There is an abundance of free-floating shame in the world, evidenced in shameful or destructive behaviors and addictions. The shame created by addictive behaviors is self-enforcing. The more shame I feel about my addiction, the more I need the addictive substance to bury the shame. Shameful or pathological behavior such as homicide is not driven by the lack of shame, but usually by an over-exposure to shame in childhood and throughout one's life.

The shamed person simply pulls the plug on his or her ability to feel shame or anything close to it such as guilt.

I met a man who was in prison for murdering two young women when he was twenty. I was in a therapeutic training group within the prison for a week with him. He was the leader of our training and I grew to know him and understand him. He described the origins of his shame and rage and homicidal ideas as coming on quite suddenly one night when he was three years old. He remembers the night his mother had him get out of the car on a disserted stretch of road. He cannot remember what she told him that night, but he could remember her face looking back at him as she drove off and left him standing in the dark.

He also remembered the terror he felt along with the shame of having such little meaning to his mother. He thought the feelings he was having were going to kill him that night. In his attempt to survive, he decided to pretend he was not terrified and ashamed. Instead he chose to feel rage and anger sufficient to get him through the night. He was found at dawn by a farmer. From there he was placed in fairly good foster homes. Yet he never adapted due to his constant anger and he never found his mother.

He did, however, find two women walking their little boys on a country road late one afternoon as he was driving home from his job. He said he cannot remember feeling anything but terror for the little boys as he pulled out his gun and shot the two mothers. He then grabbed the boys and dropped them off at the sheriff's station and turned himself in as well.

I believed I would not find respect for this man when I first met him and was perplexed by what I could learn from this trainer who was a killer. He taught me a new-found respect for the power of shame. I continued to despise his behavior but had some compassion for that scared three-year-old who never really left that dark dead-end road. My trainer in prison had internalized shame. This is the most debilitating form of shame and very seldom arises from a single event.

This is a dramatic example of the depth of sleep created by shame. There are less dramatic but still toxic interactions we may be having every day that are shameful. I see good parents, well intentioned and conscientious, inducing shame in their children with their misguided lack of awareness. Such parents often paraphrase the Bible, "Spare the rod and spoil the child." Parents sometimes think that they are doing the child a spiritual service by spanking them. I perpetuated this doctrine on my first two children with an occasional spanking, usually stemming from my fear, instead of from awareness of the limits they required at the moment.

It was not until I saw a historical documentary on sheep herders of ancient times, that I realized the role of the rod and the staff. They were used not to punish or hit the sheep, but rather to provide guidance, structure, and occasionally to prevent the sheep from walking off a cliff, as sheep supposedly tend to do. Given a new perspective, I now had greater awareness of my conflicted feelings that appeared any time I chose to not "spare the rod." This is not to say children do not need significant guidance and discipline. However punishment provides neither. Coming up with meaningful consequences seems to produce the better result on children's decisions and behaviors.

Indispensable narcissism is required to get our needs met upon our birth, since we are totally dependent on others to keep us alive or even to support our heads. The quicker our parents are in recognizing and attending to our cries of fear or discomfort or hunger, they reinforce our inherent lovability. It seems to me, impossible to spoil a baby by attending to its needs. Of course, some babies have much higher needs for comfort and attention based on their temperament.

I remember the nurses being quite concerned over the fact I could not get a bath in without my newborn daughter screaming for me the day after she was born. The staff said she was inconsolable unless I was holding her. She was my fourth child, so I could recognize the types of cries. Hers was for comfort. If I had listened to the nurses' sympathetic words or my outdated baby books, I would have viewed my daughter as a spoiled baby. She continued to cry unless held when she was awake until she was four months old.

She was diagnosed with cancer of the eye (retino-blastoma) when she was seventeen weeks old and had a series of surgeries and radiation treatments for the next two months. She stopped demanding to be held during the course of her treatments and became a calm and undemanding baby. It is as if she knew at birth that she would need an extra reserve of holding and comforting to get her through what lay ahead.

How quickly a parent recognizes a child's needs and attends to them will determine the child's lovability. The first major challenge occurs near age two when our job is to begin to define our identity as separate from our parents or primary care givers. This is done through challenging most limits and saying no even when we would like to say yes. If parents have empathy for the child they will not shame them by ridiculing their needs. It is not helpful to punish or yell at a child for saying no to you. Rather calmly let them know that while their job may be to say no, your job is to protect them.

They will not understand all the words, but they will understand your intent to honor their needs while not giving in to their wants. You will get a chance to repeat this lesson when they reach adolescence. Hopefully they will still be carrying the sign, "I am lovable and deserve to be here." Was your sign still intact when you reached junior high? If not, what tore at it?

Maintaining their lovability despite their behavior helps a child keep shame from becoming internalized. Forms of shame include physical, verbal, or emotional abuse. All challenge our sense of lovability. Sexual abuse or incest seems to have the most shaming impact because it comes with a powerful double message. "I love you. Therefore I will use you for my desire."

Comparisons with other children, boundary violations such as treating a child like a buddy, or having the child perform beyond their emotional capacity are potentially shaming behaviors. Sometimes shaming behaviors happen far away from a parent's view, such as on the school playground or at the hand of siblings who are babysitting. I am not an opponent of having siblings provide anything more than short-term care for a younger child. I have heard way too many stories of brothers or sisters teasing and ridiculing their siblings. The younger sibling may not respect the authority of the older one watching him, which is a recipe for abuse, as the older one tries to establish control. Given the naturally competitive nature between siblings, unless there is a significant age difference of more than five years, they do not make the most nurturing caregivers. There are exceptions to this, as in the case of early-developed, empathic children.

I also work with a lot of people who were literally tormented by their peers, usually sometime in elementary or junior high school. This can have a long-term effect on a child's sense of self. It can create significant feelings of shame, especially if there has been prior damage to the banner of lovability within us. To those who carry the shame of childhood bullying, often with feelings of being the only one bullied, I wish to tell you, you are not alone. There are many others who were treated as cruelly as you. There was nothing remotely wrong with them either. They were victims, too, of children asleep to feelings of empathy but not to shame. Often we assume incorrectly, that if we were bullied or picked on, it was about something wrong with us, instead of something absent or harmed in the bully.

If we are exposed to external shame often enough and long enough and our banner of esteem becomes torn away, we then start the process of internalizing shame. We begin to replace the sense of "I deserve to be here and be loved" with "I am bad and do not deserve to be here." This process usually starts when we develop defenses to keep the overwhelming feelings of shame at bay. Early defenses usually include blaming others, rage, self-consciousness, and perfectionist tendencies.

Condescension toward others, often compounded with the desire for power, are common trademarks of shame and the recipe for creating a bully.

Identity development and boundary formation halt when internalized shame starts to activate self-destructive behaviors such as drug use, self-punishment, promiscuity, and a host of other ways to destroy the self that no longer "deserves to be here." Much of what I describe here about the concepts of shame comes from working with the framework first identified by Gershen Kaufman in the book, *Shame: The Power of Caring*.

One way to determine the level of shame you may have acquired is to consider the quality of your inner dialogues or the nature of your inner voice. Is it loving and supportive even when you make mistakes? Or does it have a critical and non-accepting attitude toward you.

Another powerful tool for waking up is to develop awareness of your inner voice and its disposition toward you. Waking up can mean realizing that we may be interacting with ourselves from a shame-based perspective. This can give us a new choice. We can start interacting with ourselves from a more nurturing and effective responsibility-based style. This shift can go a long way to restoring our sense of worth and right to be here. Imagine how damaging it may be to our self-worth to have a constant critical voice with in us. Take a moment to reflect on the type of interactions you have within yourself. Do you recognize the voice?

Responsibility-based dialogue focuses on your behaviors that need attention, not on your personhood or self-value. Your right to have needs along with imperfections is respected instead of attacked or devalued. Are your inner dialogues and thoughts focused on the goal of change or do they focus on the goal of punishment?

Responsibility focuses on the question of what we need in order to learn and grow versus how well we are performing. Shame-based dialogues offer little redemption from our wickedness. Our responsibility to ourselves will find a way back to self-acceptance through learning from our mistakes. Despite possible feelings of anger, responsibility-based interactions allow us to take full ownership of our feelings and encourage connection and intimacy with others. Shame-based interactions blame our feelings of rage onto others and shift the resolution to them, which invites alienation and emotional isolation.

Extending the dialogue with ourselves to how we interact with others can also be a step toward waking up. Is your work setting shame-based or does it promote personal responsibility? Which style were you parented with? How did you parents handle you mistakes? How do you parent? If your five-year-old child spills her milk at the dinner table after you directed her to move her cup, how do you respond? In a shame-based system, a parent reinforces her mistake with a statement such as, "I told you so," or a scolding. A responsible parent tells her, "I trust you know where the towel is." This is often more effective in our overall goal of increasing the child's sense of worth and industriousness. Is that your overall goal in parenting? Or did this reasonable method get buried under something else?

I want to assure parents reading this that there is significant room for both trial and error along with redemption in the way we parent our children. The ability to maintain a feeling of connection to the parent despite the use of punishment is critical in stopping the internalization of shame. A sense of "a collapsing bridge" or feeling utterly alone allows shame to take hold.

To illustrate this point, I am reminded of an incident with my four-year-old son. One day, chasing a squirrel, he ran right in front of me, out into the street, and right in front of a car! The driver narrowly missed him. I was scared out of my senses and ran out to pick him up and gave him a swat on the behind. When we reached the curb, I set him down. I had a choice. I could leave him at the curb to feel the consequences for his behavior and walk away. I chose to not punish him any further. Instead, I hugged him and apologized for spanking him. I said I had been scared and thought he was going to get hit by the car. I maintained my connection with him. I did not let the "bridge collapse" by abandoning him at a time when he was also scared.

Parents are the primary source of security and love for children. No matter what they do, children need to have a sense of an everlasting, emotional bridge with their parents. We can ease a lot of the mistakes we make as parents if we maintain both humility and our connection of love with our children.

> Big heartedness is the most important virtue on the spiritual journey.
> —Matthew Fox, Author

Another note on shame. Sometimes the feeling of shame attaches itself like a sponge onto specific emotions we experience early in life. This can be overwhelming in adulthood, when we experience certain feelings and "just want to die." When shame attaches itself to grief, some people having difficulty leaving unfulfilling relationships. Our first major loss may be accompanied by a belief that we weren't good enough to keep the relationship. If a child looses a parent, from death or divorce, the child often feels both grief and shame. I call this the *major abandonment emotion* or the "endless black abyss." Avoiding these unresolved feelings can grow to control much of our behavior in relationships.

I watched in semi-detached agony as my son struggled with this feeling after the collapse of his first romantic relationship with a sweet sixteen-year-old girl. She was a year older than he was and had decided to break up with him to return to her former, violent boyfriend. My son not only felt strong grief for loosing the relationship, but also felt shame for not being good enough to keep her affection. Compounding the shame was the fact that the other boyfriend had been so cruel to her. I found my son, doubled over on his bed, moaning in pain, asking me why feelings were so painful and if they could kill a person.

I did not have a good answer that day for my child, a six foot one, starting, football center who had seemed immune to physical pain. I just sat on his bed and told him to breath through the pain. I was in pain as well, because I knew his feelings of loss and grief were going to be intertwined with the sense of shame for a while, no matter what I said and no matter how long I sat by his bed.

Waking up from shameful feelings involves increasing our awareness and gaining a deeper perspective on the causes. Since shame happened in the context of a relationship, my son required compassion from another relationship to help him resolve it. Shameful feelings thrive in secret and we sometimes go to great lengths to hide them.

I once had the opportunity to work side by side with a delightful and dedicated nun who told me her experience with shame. One evening, she was driving home from a movie. A man ran out in the street when she stopped at a dark intersection and jumped in her car. He then had her pull over in a parking lot where he raped her at knifepoint and stole her wallet. For years she carried in secret the shame that belonged to the rapist. Her overwhelming shame and fear distorted her thinking. She believed her two mistakes—going to a movie on a week night and stopping at the intersection—were the reasons for her rape. She was too ashamed to go to confession or take the sacraments and considered leaving her community. It was through her volunteer work at the hospital that she found relief.

She was counseling and offering spiritual support to a young woman who had been raped. The woman also described the mistake she made of getting in her car after dark in her employee parking lot. Healing occurred as the nun courageously told the woman what had happened to her. In seeing the innocence of the other victim, she was able to finally give witness to her own.

Exposing Shame

> If you bring forth what is within you, what you bring forth will save you. If you do not

bring forth what is within you, what you
do not bring forth will destroy you.
—Gospel of St Thomas, Saying 70

Shame needs to be exposed in order to heal. Finding a loving person or a friend to share your secrets
with is often a powerful catalyst for finding inner
freedom. As shame is such a prevailing force in
addictions, most recovery programs, including the
twelve-step program ask people to "take a thor-
ough moral inventory" of themselves and their lives
and share the results with one other person. Further
steps ask for "amends" or taking responsibility for
the harm we may have done to others by shame-
induced sleep. Often the majority of amends will
need to be with oneself. Most people I see are by
far the most insensitive to themselves.

This process of exposure and awareness allows
shame to shift into guilt. Remember, guilt can be
healthy and energizing and allows us to feel our
conscience again. Eventually the most shameful secrets we have about ourselves can be
transformed into guilt and finally reasonable
regret. This takes courage. However, the reward is
compassion.

Another area to explore in addressing shame is
within our relationships. We seem to seek out people
of similar shame levels and self-esteem. Therefore,
as we grow in our awareness, we may start seeing ways we shame others. Awareness creates

additional opportunities and options for choice. It is our responsibility to consider our thoughts and emotions and then to make wiser choices. We may also see that others are shaming or attempting to diminish us. This will give us the opportunity to set boundaries and define the quality of relationships we desire.

COMPASSION

> Compassion is the ultimate and most meaningful emotional embodiment of emotional maturity. It is through compassion that a person achieves the highest peak and the deepest reach in his or her search for self-fulfillment.
> ——Arthur Jersild, Child psychologist

The last step in resolving shame is to develop and maintain a strong nurturing relationship with ourselves. If we suffered parental deprivation, it is our responsibility to re-parent and find aspects of ourselves that may have gone into hiding. This can be simply stated as "acting with compassion" versus "re-acting" to shameful triggers. Remember, we need direction, guidance, safety, structure, and acceptance to fully mature and wake up. Acting with compassion is sometimes called *compassionate self-discipline* and requires motivating ourselves from our innate spirit without using fear and punishment. Punishment of the self will later often lead to self-indulgent or narcissistic behavior.

In transforming ourselves back to our original birth-right of "I am lovable and I deserve to be here," we now have the freedom to let people get close to us. We no longer have to fear them finding out who we really are inside.

> I was a neurotic for years. I was anxious and depressed and selfish. Everyone kept telling me to change. I resented them, I agreed with them, and I wanted to change, but simply couldn't, no matter how hard I tried. What hurt the most was that, like the others, my best friend kept insisting that I change. So I felt powerless and trapped. Then one day, he said to me, "Don't change. I love you just as you are." These words were music to my ears: "Don't change. Don't change. Don't change... I love you as you are." I relaxed. I came alive. And suddenly I changed! Now I know that I couldn't really change until I found someone who would love me whether I changed or not.
> —Anthony de Mello *The Song of the Bird*

This level of compassion and understanding for the self, which Anthony de Mello describes, is the reward for resolving shame. It is the compassion I regret not having shown all the people that have crossed my path.

SECTION THREE
STAYING AWAKE

ANOTHER SUFI STORY.

A mullah was walking along the road when he saw a lion in with a herd of sheep. The lion was not attacking the sheep, indeed, the lion was acting like a sheep. The mullah asked the lion, "What are you doing acting like a frightened sheep?"

The Lion responded, "I am a sheep; I have always been a sheep."

This is a disturbing situation thought the mullah, who then stated, "Can you not see that you are a King, not a cowering sheep?"

The lion said, "I am a sheep, why do you think I am a lion? If I were a lion, the sheep would be scared of me, therefore I must be a sheep."

The mullah was not going to give up. He grabbed the Lion by the neck and dragged him over to a pool of water and said, "There, see for yourself! You are a lion!"

The lion looked at his reflection in disbelief. Finally he stated, "Mullah, you are right, I am a lion. What do I do now?"

What do you suppose the lion chose to do after he woke up to his true identity? Why do some people appear to start to wake up then retreat even further back into the delusion of self-righteousness, claiming they have found the truth? I watch so many people seeking one spiritual workshop after another, attending countless seminars on self-enlightenment. Yet often they do not stay awake for long. Staying awake does require a commitment to explore the endless possibilities of your potential. It is also a commitment to perpetually examine and expand your perceptions of yourselves, others, and life itself with humility and tolerance.

Maintaining a level of awareness in our life involves developing and maintaining relationships. The first relationship that is essential to maintain is our relationship to our self. This involves finding our way back to our essence or origin, which for many is spiritual. Often our relationship to spirit has been affected by many factors. We need to examine these factors from a mature perspective versus throwing out our concepts of spirit entirely, because we might disagree with organized religion. There are tools that can aid in this process.

This final section describes some of those tools. Note this is the final section, not the first section, for a reason. Many people I have worked with over the years have inadvertently used spiritual or religious tools without rigorous self-examination and understanding. This shortcut can lead to knowledge without character or compassion, void of true wisdom. This is not usually sustainable or satisfying for long. Spiritual or religious development left unchecked by the humility of self-awareness can inadvertently lead to self-aggrandizement. It can also lead to terrorism if coupled with fear and shamelessness.

The reward for staying awake is a much deeper understanding of the depth of your nature and the quality of your relationships. Intimacy with self, others, and life grows if we continue to strive for awareness through self-examination with some of the tools outlined in this section.

> I tried to die near the end of the war. The same dream returned each night until I dared not go to sleep and grew quite ill. I dreamed I had a child, and even in the dream I saw it was my life, and it was an idiot, and I ran away. But it always crept onto my lap again, clutched at my clothes. Until I thought, if I could kiss it, what ever in it was my own, perhaps I could sleep. And I bent to its broken face, and it was horrible...but I kissed it. I think one must finally take one's life in one's arms."
> —Holga in *After the Fall* by Arthur Miller

CHAPTER NINE
SPIRITUALITY AND RELIGION

DIFFERENTIATING

Spirituality tends to broadly encompass our relationship to this life. It may be our meaning, our mission or our purpose or simply what gets us out of bed in the morning. Spiritual identity formation is fundamental to waking up and essential to maintaining a drive for awareness. It encompasses our reason to live and provides the energy necessary to fight the gravitational pull of entropy.

Spirituality is very different from religiosity. I make this distinction due to the fact that the majority of people I have worked with over the years describe being significantly injured by organized religion. Some describe damage occurring from the doctrine or dogma of their childhood religion. Others describe feeling hurt by the intolerant views of leaders within their religion. A few individuals simply cannot believe holy books are anything but fairy tales designed to take away nighttime fears. Regardless of their source of perceived injury, it is often necessary to examine this source in order to develop a healthy spiritual identity.

In order to separate spirituality from religion, it is helpful to understand their differences. Religions often have doctrine, prescribed holy days, food laws, sacred books, appointed leaders, and rituals. They regularly follow cultural and sometimes geographic guidelines. Most religions describe the soul's journey upon death and the behavior necessary to direct this passage. Vast numbers of people may share the same religious viewpoints and maintain a strong community of support and fellowship.

Spirituality, on the other hand, is self-defined and self-examined in terms of what is holy. No two people share exactly the same spiritual views just as no two people walk through this life on the very same road. A spiritual person seeks to understand the intent or meaning of religious doctrine beyond its literal interpretation.

I have worked with people who describe themselves as religious, but have little personalized spiritual identity. I have worked with people I would describe as highly developed in their spiritual characteristics who have no formal religious affiliation. People can also spiritualize their religious beliefs in order to strengthen them. This often comes about through exploring and examining one's religion and seeking the truth that resonates within it. Duality, which is found in most religions, is often challenged when assessing spirituality and replaced with attempts at finding internal unity.

Spiritual Maturation

> Oh, what a catastrophe, what a maiming of love when it was made a personal, merely personal feeling, taken away from the rising and the setting of the sun, and cut off from the magical connection of the solstice and the equinox!...
>
> We are bleeding at the roots, because we are cut off from the earth and the sun and the stars, and love is a grinning mockery, because, poor blossom, we plucked it from its stem on the tree of Life, and expected it to keep on blooming in our civilized vase on the table.
> —D. L. Lawrence

The process of spiritual maturity happens sometimes through questioning one's childhood religion and, in doing so, making it your own. Hand-me-down religious beliefs do not work for many people, especially independent thinkers, who are willing to risk their soul in search of the truth.

When I read about those of great faith from either a religion or spiritual practice, I see a common element of maturity. Most have dared to challenge their childhood views of a black-and-white or good-and-bad religion and have moved into the adolescent phase of defiance and questioning. Through the process of doubting, they often find their true faith and tend to move into a more mature view of religion. This enables them to separate out the people who may have hurt them from the doctrines of their childhood faith. Just as we need to differentiate or separate from our parents' identity in order to have our own personality, so we need to develop spiritual or religious maturity. You may have very well separated defiantly from your parents' religion, but this is only the beginning of the process.

Have you begun the journey of finding your spiritual identity? For those of you who adhere to the religion of your childhood, ask simply, do I adhere out of fear or apathy or challenged faith? Ask yourself why? Nothing I have observed keeps people deeper in sleep than blind, unquestioned and unconscious faith. Blind faith lives up to its name and is responsible for unquestioned wars and unspeakable acts of cruelty.

The following story of Uncle Ralph illustrates the concept of spiritual or religious immaturity, which relies on an all-knowing and magical parent figure, ready to rescue us from self-responsibility.

> Uncle Ralph was a self-described "man of God" and attended church every Sunday with Aunt Sylvia. They lived near the banks of the Red River in Fargo, North Dakota. The river began to flood one spring day

after a winter of unusually heavy snow. Dikes were built to try to save the town, however, they were about to break this night. Aunt Ellen, who lived in New Mexico, heard about the dikes leaking on CNN and immediately called Aunt Sylvia to tell her to evacuate. Aunt Sylvia woke up Uncle Ralph to pack and leave. He helped her pack up their large Cadillac to the roof, but told her he was not leaving as God would save him. Aunt Sylvia tried to get him to change his mind but knew he was a stubborn man. Her arguments were pointless in the face of his faith. She drove off minutes before the dikes finally broke. She found her neighbor Eddy, who had a boat, and asked him to go pick up her husband. Eddy found Ralph leaning out the second floor window of his house surrounded by the river and asked Ralph to crawl in. Ralph said, "No, God will save me."

Eddy protested, but he had no effect on Ralph's determination to have God save him. As the floodwater rose, Ralph was forced to the roof top. Aunt Sylvia was not going to give up on her husband. She went to the evacuation headquarters and told them about her stranded husband. They routed a National Guard helicopter to fetch Ralph off the roof. When the helicopter threw Ralph a life ring to climb into, he refused and said, "Go rescue someone else, God will save me." Eventually the floodwater washed Uncle Ralph off the roof and he drowned immediately as he could not swim a stroke. When Uncle Ralph arrived in heaven, he asked God, "Why did you not save me?"

God shook his head and said, "Ralph, I sent Ellen, I sent Eddy, and, hell, I even sent the National Guard to save you! What were you thinking, Ralph?"
—"What Were You Thinking Uncle Ralph" Concept taken from "The Grapevine," an AA publication

Once one has differentiated themselves from their original childhood religious or spiritual injuries through self-examination and awareness, they are then free to choose or reject religious or spiritual principles based on their true self rather than out of residual anger or fear or indoctrination. This is to me the highest form of religious freedom that few take the risk or time to achieve.

In ancient cultural practices, Eastern philosophies and twelve-step programs there are several spiritual tools, which are universal to all religions and paths of greater awareness.

Replacing Fear with Faith

I discussed the twelve-step's first step earlier, which leads us to a position of humility—a qualification for any type of change or growth. Humbly surrendering to our humanity compels us to reach out to others for assistance in waking up to ourselves. Thus the second step, "Came to believe that a power greater than ourselves could restore us to sanity."

A single reading of this second step may not be sufficient to see its many inherent tools. They are better illuminated through breaking the step down in phrases and phases.

"Came to believe" is a process not an event and basically requires us to first come or show up. It may be to come to a twelve-step meeting or to take ten minutes for self-reflection. If we show up often enough, eventually we start to "come to" or gain awareness and perspective on some of our thoughts and behaviors. As this process of self-reflection or self-examination continues within the context of relationships or twelve-step meetings or awareness-promoting groups, we come to believe.

We began to see that there is something greater than our intellect or emotions in leading us to freedom and wisdom. This "power greater than ourselves" does not have to be a god or religion, but it can be. It can also be the powerful force that comes from compassion and understanding from others, when we expose our true nature to them. Restoration to sanity happens when we stop repeating destructive patterns. Insanity has been often defined at twelve-step meetings as "repeating the same destructive behavior over and over again, each time expecting a different result."

Insanity can also be the inability to see our injuries and how we inflict them on others. "Being restored to sanity" often means finding and believing in a force capable of allowing us to forgive ourselves. The second step in its simple words outlines the process of finding faith in something other than our fears.

Ben was only fourteen when I met him in adolescent treatment for his drug addiction. He had experienced chronic illnesses all through his short life and had no need for or belief in a higher power. I was quite direct in my approach in my early days and told him to find something, besides himself that he could believe in by the end of the day. He chose his hot chocolate mug during dinner. He said to me, "If I need to believe in something greater than myself, this is going to have to be it." I said to his surprise that the mug was an excellent choice and informed him he needed to carry it with him to his twelve-step meetings and group therapy sessions. Each time he returned from his meetings he would describe what the mug experienced. At first his higher power mug experienced only new people and new ideas, but he agreed that this may very well be the higher power he needed.

This was a huge step for him in developing trust! Over the course of a month, he was able to expand his belief in his mug to include concepts of friendship and caring. At his graduation from treatment he eloquently described how he "came to believe" in the love and guidance of others as his higher power."

CHAPTER TEN
SPIRITUAL DEVELOPMENT TOOLS

There are only two ways to live your life. One is as though nothing is a miracle. The other is as though everything is a miracle.
—Albert Einstein

MEDITATION

Many describe prayer as asking for guidance from the divine and meditation as listening for the answer. Commonly meditation is defined as the practice of focusing the mind and often the body with a specific routine. It encompasses a far-reaching number of both spiritual and religious practices as well as secular activities such as the martial arts. There are many forms of meditation to choose from for enhancing both secular and spiritual growth. I will focus on the following forms that I have found especially helpful in enhancing emotional insight and physical wellbeing. These are very easy to practice on a daily basis.

MINDFULNESS

Take a moment to reflect on your most joyful moments. What do these moments in time have in

common? Often the times we experience eupho-
ria are linked by our total focus in the moment. We
often are fully present and at least partially awake
for those big events in our life, such as the birth of our
children. In our attempt to freeze these moments in
our memory, we experience a heightened state of
awareness. Think of the spiritual quality or holiness
we could add to our life if we chose to be mindful most of the time instead of just for those great
events!

I sometimes reflect on those moments I have lost
with my children because I was busy planning the
next meal or thinking about something else while
nursing or playing with them. However I did manage to catch a few of them and they are more
valuable than any digital picture I have carefully
placed in albums and shoeboxes. One particular mindful moment occurred at 5:30 in the morning when I was feeling slightly exhausted and very
put out by my newborn son's hourly feedings. I
was sitting in a rocker looking out on the patio as
I nursed him and realized it was a glorious sum-
mer morning complete with a pair of blue birds
serenading us. I became nearly mindful in that
moment and realized life is holy and does not get
any better than this moment, complete with a
new life nursing at my breast. This was quite a shift
from my resentful non-mindful state and brought
with it a most cherished gift of a fully preserved
moment.

There was another minute, one October, which I was able to fully capture and experience. I was sitting on a Sanibel Island beach on a beautiful but ominously overcast day, the day before Hurricane Wilma came to shore. I was reading a good book, when I felt the need to look around. I saw my two boys, one twenty-six and one sixteen, busy building a fort in the sand. I became mindful of the moment—mindful that they were my sons, mindful that their shoulders rubbed together without self-consciousness. I was mindful of the laughter coming from my son who had been in the sandstorms of Iraq. I was mindful of the love and respect pouring on him from my other son's eyes. I was instantly euphoric and asked myself," why"?

I often ask "why" and then collapse the state of mindfulness. It was heaven on earth for those few moments because I was capturing most of what the moment contained. It was a moment of creation, love, choices, joy, connections, rich with history, all coming together in the moment.

Mindfulness is simply about being fully present in the moment. Simple, but not easy with all the distractions we have today. It means capturing all that life has to offer one moment at a time. Sometimes it means turning off the video game and getting outside to experience something new, or experiencing something new in something old. Reminding the self to fully show up periodically increases our state of mindfulness. A question I sometimes ask to facilitate this awareness is, "What is this moment meant to teach me?" Then I try to stop thinking and just observe.

WALKING

For many, walking is a natural form of mediation. The desire to walk for clarity and insight has been prescribed by many of the great masters. Indigenous Native Americans walked for their vision quests. Jesus, according to biblical records, walked in the desert for forty days and forty nights to "awaken" to his path. The natural rhythm or action in walking has long provided those with poetic or mystic endowments the ability to dissolve the attachments and worries of this earth. In our walking we can loosen the fears of ourselves to the wisdom of ourselves.

I teach workshops to assist in creativity. One of the essential tasks I assign is to walk daily to nourish both the body and the soul. The ebb and flow and seasons of life are most closely experienced through even a short daily walk outside. A useful source of ideas and formalized workshops on creativity can be found in Julia Cameron's book, *The Vein of Gold*.

> I now know that I am not alone in believing that walking with our soles is really walking

with our souls....We walk into expanded possibility: If you can bear it, the soles of our feet lead us to the feats of our souls.
—Julia Cameron, *The Vein of Gold*

SELF OBSERVATION

Self-observation or objectively witnessing our thoughts, feelings, and behaviors can greatly enhance our awareness or internal vision. The key to effective self-observation is to be objective and detached. I sometimes have to envision in my mind that I am watching some other woman dressed like me on a TV screen. Judgments and criticism impose strong barriers between most people and maintaining this kind of objectivity. The minute I start judging myself, I will seek justification or other defenses and all objectivity is gone.

I, personally, think I experience a loss of approximately thirty IQ points or more when I become angry or frightened. If I can move myself into a position of self-observation, I can usually restore my mental functioning. This is not always easy and sometimes involves taking a deep breath and shifting my perspective at the same time. The shift that works for me is to imagine I am sitting on the moon with a telescope observing the woman dressed like me. I know it is working if I start laughing at my self-created drama.

Self-observation leads to self-knowledge. Self-knowledge leads to greater knowledge and understanding of others. Greater understanding of others eliminates fear and leads to compassion. It would be difficult to create war or violence or pockets of hunger if compassion dominated societies. It all starts with observing the self, something you can do right now.

Seek Higher Ground

If you were a boy scout or girl scout, you may have been taught this basic survival concept. It is also a potent spiritual tool as well. When we are lost in the woods or anywhere, often the wisest thing to do is to seek the highest vantage point. From a higher perspective we are able to see more landmarks. The same applies when we are feeling lost or simply need a perspective adjustment. Seeking higher ground almost always means addressing our fears. One of my favorite questions for putting fear in its place is, "What is the worst thing than can happen?" If I get a scary response such as, "someone might die." I then ask for directions or assistance from someone I trust.

If we grew up in deprivation or did not build a trusting relationship to a higher power, we tend to imagine that situations will turn out awful and we loose perspective very quickly with the first rush of fear. Seeking higher ground emotionally by reducing fear, seeking it mentally through questioning our judgment of the situation, and seeking it spiritually by reaching out to others for their perspective can expand our view greatly. This can be especially helpful for those times of high anxiety, which can greatly distort our ability to perceive accurately.

Reframing and Detaching

I especially enjoy reframing as a spiritual tool. It allows us to seek both a balanced and imaginative perspective at the same time. Reframing involves putting a different lens on a situation, which can be very helpful if we have trust issues or struggle with despair. I choose how to view most situations automatically from my past or from a state of unawareness. In reframing I consciously choose how to view my situation. This in no way alters reality. It alters my mood and my attitude. It offers me more choices in how I respond to a situation. I like choices.

One way to reframe is to view a problem as a challenge to develop your character. So you owe four-thousand dollars in taxes this year. This could be a problem for most of us. If you detach from it, or remove your judgments of yourself and the government, you now have the energy to consider all the options in a more creative way. Remember, fear and judgment block creativity. This is why we can often give great advice to others but not to ourselves.

Reframing also works in resolving difficulties in relationships. Imagine that your current struggles in relationships are with the "perfect" people—people who can help you recreate feelings or situations you experienced as a child. Now imagine that you have the opportunity to resolve these feelings once and for all. Your controlling boss now becomes a respected guide on your journey back to your source of mistrust of authority. This time you have a whole different set of skills and awareness and, most of all, choices.

There is a lovely parable about our enemy in the book by Neale Donald Walsch called *The Little Soul and the Sun*. In this children's story an angel is struggling to experience of forgiveness. Unfortunately, all is well in his part of heaven. Nothing to forgive, so his very best friend decides to help him by coming to earth with him and being his angry enemy. The only thing his friend asks of him at the moment he strikes out is to "remember who I really am." I have found this phrase very useful in detaching from people whom I initially see as vexations to my spirit. Over time, we often see that those individuals whom we initially find objectionable give us far more opportunity for character reflection and growth than those we like or admire. So remember who your enemy really is.

I once worked with a very gentle and compassionate psychiatrist who exhibited great skill intervening for women in abusive relationships. Due to their learned helplessness and high dependency needs, getting women to leave these relationships in order to save their life and limbs can be quite difficult.

I asked Doctor Sands what his "magic" therapy entailed. He said simply, "Since these women over idolize their husband and see him as God, I advise them to replace his face with a face they most fear, often a cobra snake." He smiled, "This usually breaks the spell."

Reframing can also assist us in doing that which we think we cannot do. Imagine if you were only using 10 percent of your brain and you found a way to wake up the other 90 percent. What could you do? Keeping in mind the Sufi story, imagine you were raised by loving parents who simply did not see that you were a "lion". What if these parents did not know what you were capable of becoming?

I remember reading a story by Joseph C. Pearce a long time ago in his book, *The Magical Child*. He described working in his woodshop one night when his preschool child came down to say good night. His son accidentally got in the way of a flying piece of wood and severed an artery in his little arm. As he desperately tries to stop the blood loss and calculates the drive to the hospital, he screams out, "You have to stop the bleeding!" His son, who has always trusted his father, assumes this is a command and immediately stops his "involuntary" loss of blood.

I understand this kind of desperation, especially when it involves children. One evening in March, I saw a TV program interrupted with flashes over Baghdad. The war in Iraq had started, my stomach turned over. I knew my son, a Marine reservist from Minnesota, was crossing the boarder into Iraq as I watched the screen in horror. I also knew I could not physically endure the emotional helplessness I was feeling for my first born in that moment. I decided to write my son a letter on how to become invisible. I had, after all, raised him with such imaginative notions of human potential. I knew of shamans of the indigenous populations of Bolivia who were quite good at creating the illusion of invisibility.

I spent the next few days studying shamanic tools and crafted the instructions to my son. I sent the letter off and I made it though the war. My son also made it through the war, but my letter never arrived; only the pink envelope I sent it in. The letter may have been censored or destroyed for whatever reason. However, its mission for me had been accomplished.

JOURNALING

Most people are highly resistant to journaling. I think too many of us were given the task as homework before we were able to imagine its value for generating self-knowledge and self-awareness. I do not think we need to journal daily to benefit from this tool. However, some discipline in writing our thoughts and feelings down on a regular basis can be very rewarding. With journaling we begin to see the cycles and patterns of our behavior and catch glimpses at the nature of our soul.

I started journaling at the age of ten. I have not done it daily and tend to be an eleventh-hour journal writer. I've journaled through pain and fear and often forget to write when life is well. People reading my journals might think I am a rather despairing creature. However, I know that at the conclusion of my painful entries on loss or disappointment, there has always been a greater restoration of my soul, even though I neglect to record it. It is also startling to me that the questions I seek answers for today are the same ones I was asking at age ten. Some things deep in us do not change or change very slowly. I believe they represent our essence. Journaling helps us identify, understand, and nourish our essential being.

Third Step Tool

The tool I would like to conclude with is the universal third step of twelve-step programs. It uses the following words to convey its many principles, "Made a decision to turn my life and my will over to the care of the God (higher power) of my understanding."

Before my adolescent, self-proclaimed agnostic clients could bolt for the door after hearing this step, I would attempt to let them know that this was not a step of conversion. Rather it is a step toward power through surrender. I would ask them to consider that neither their ego nor emotions may be the end-all resource for directing their life. Considering how fragile, sensitive, and easily frightened our egos are, we can quickly be overwhelmed with life if the ego is in charge. My ego can regress to the state of a three-year-old upon some major provocation. My emotional state is dependent on an assortment of variables.

Making a decision to surrender both our life and our will to something greater than our ego brings strength. It does not display weakness. The "God or higher power" of our understanding can be anything from a religious belief system to a set of principles or morals for conducting our life. Sometimes it can be found in a question, such as, "What is the most loving thing to do for all involved?" In maintaining awareness or spiritual growth, it is essential that we have something more stable than our ego to turn to for objective balance and guidance.

When I get on a plane I turn my life over to the care of the pilot and crew. It makes for a more restful ride. I usually peak in on them, before they lock the door, to make sure they are older then my youngest child and appear to be emotionally intact. We can choose to maintain our illusion of control, which is often accompanied by fear or anxiety. Or we can recognize how little control we really have in most situations and trust. Trust in what? For the religious person the answer is often defined in doctrine. For the agnostic or atheist it is individually defined, usually after much doubt, questioning, and exploration. Many atheists I have met are quite invested in, even obsessed with, finding the answers to this question.

This process is called "letting go" in Alcoholics Anonymous. It is also called "letting go" in several Eastern practices. Sometimes, I need to start with simply "letting it be." The energy spent trying to control external forces in our lives can be much more productive if it is directed toward internal responsibility. "I am responsible for managing my life this far" is different from controlling it.

Another example in "letting go" can be found in how we react to waiting for test results. If I am unable to let go of my illusion of control, I will ruminate and worry about the test results till they arrive. This will in no way affect the results but will greatly affect the quality of my life and relationships while waiting.

Another principle contained in this step is the concept of choosing what we need to do versus what we want to do. Generally our needs are defined as elements or behaviors essential for our growth and liberty. Our wants can often, but not always, be defined as the elements or behaviors that discourage our growth or liberty. Every time we choose our needs over our wants we develop discipline and trust. Discipline is like our muscles. When it is used, it is strengthened. When it is disregarded, it atrophies. This can be a difficult spiritual tool, especially if we were raised without discipline or worse, with too much. However, it is another essential aspect of growing up and staying awake.

The benefit of living a life of choosing what you need versus what you want is that, eventually, they become the same. Every time an addict attends an Alcoholics Anonymous meeting that they need, versus drinking or staying home as they want, their recovery and strength grow.

I believe the strongest form of self-love comes from choosing what we need versus what we want for ourselves. I also believe the highest expression of love is choosing to act in loving ways even when we do not feel loving. It is easy to love when it is fueled by emotion. It is equally important to love out of a choice we make to ourselves despite the lack of feeling.

CHAPTER ELEVEN
INTIMACY AND RELATIONSHIP SKILLS

MATURE LOVE

I believe the most satisfying and expanding human experience is that of creating mature love. Granted, the infatuation of immature love can be more intense, but it does not necessarily produce growth. Immature love tends to look to another person for their wholeness and self-identity. Mature love has gone through the "dark night of the soul." This has started the journey in waking up. Mature lovers no longer search for wholeness in others because they are finding it within themselves. They seek completeness through intimacy in relationships.

Intimacy is the expression of love both for the self and for others. It is the reward for waking up and the most powerful tool for staying awake. Intimacy requires that we interact with another human being with authenticity. To do this, three elements are helpful. The first one involves knowing who you really are—understanding your defenses, patterns of relating, and having some awareness of your intent for the relationship.

The second element is maintaining who you really are. This requires not only knowing who you are but also having the emotional boundaries to maintain your full identity within a relationship. The third element essential for intimacy is to share who you really are. This involves taking risks and exposing both your dark side and your dreams. As a dear friend would say to me, "Friends know and accept the good, the bad, and the ugly within us."

There are several detrimental myths in our society regarding intimacy. One is the belief that one person can fulfill all our intimacy needs. This belief is more a prerequisite for dependent relationships than the healthy, interdependent kind.

TYPES OF INTIMACY

We all have more than seven different types of intimacy needs and we give each varying degrees of emphasis. Nine different types of intimacy were originally identified by Marilyn Mason, an author, speaker and management consultant..

It would be unrealistic to expect one or even two people to fulfill all our intimacy needs. We actually need several people in our life to fulfill both our healthy interdependency and intimacy needs. Very few of us are taught the significance of having what I call, "our chicken soup support system." These are the people who will bring us food even when we are contagious. They are the people we can call in the middle of the night. They may be parents, siblings, best friends, or a spouse. To function at a high level of interdependency with adequate support, our support system should have a minimum of four and preferably six people. These four to six people create our inner circle of intimate resources. We also need an additional outer circle of friends and acquaintances as resources we can pull into our inner circle. The number and variety of persons in this outer circle depends on the stability of our inner circle as well as our personal preferences. Introverts may only need a handful of friends in this outer circle. Extroverts may have dozens.

The other myth is that intimacy is limited to sexual relationships. Physical intimacy is only one intimate area and can include both sexual and affectionate contact. A nursing mother may be getting all her sexual and affectionate intimacy needs met through breast feeding. People in a celibate state can get their physical intimacy needs met by giving and receiving affectionate hugs or nurturing touch.

Other areas of intimacy include recreational, emotional, social, spiritual, aesthetic, and intellectual. We all vary in which areas are most important. I know wives who do not appreciate the value of recreational intimacy their husbands share with their sport buddies. A few men, on the other hand, struggle with valuing the social intimacy women experience while chatting or shopping together.

The most misunderstood genders values revolve around physical intimacy. Men generally prefer sexual intimacy with some affectionate intimacy in order to feel loved. Women, I have observed, prefer affectionate intimacy with some sexual intimacy to feel loved. Just a minor variation, but it is responsible for many hurt feelings. When we confront such misunderstandings, the key to resolution is to communicate our thoughts and feelings. Communication increases awareness, offers choices, and gives us the ability to negotiate compassionately.

Intellectual intimacy comes in many forms and is created by sharing our thoughts and ideas with others. We may need several people in our lives to bounce ideas off of or to engage in political discussions or to evaluate current events. I know of several strong platonic relationships between men and women built primarily on intellectual intimacy. This can be threatening to a partner if who does not share a similar drive for intellectual intimacy.

Emotional intimacy generally is limited to a few close friends, relatives, and our partners. With these people we can be vulnerable in both exposing and expressing our feelings. Emotional intimacy often is desired from our primary relationship, but this not essential for a stable marriage. I have observed several secure marriages in which one or both of the partners will not regularly disclose feelings. Yet these marriage can work when both partners accept and are comfortable with their differences. Some partners choose to get their emotional needs fulfilled with close friends.

Spiritual intimacy can be shared with other people, animals, and nature. It involves a sense of oneness or core connection to life's meaning with another life form. Several people I know feel spiritual intimacy with the ocean or the mountains. This can be a problem for primary relationships if one partner experiences this kind of intimacy in the context of a religious community and the other does not. Again, the key to resolution is awareness of its importance within the partnership or marriage.

Aesthetic intimacy comes from sharing music, creative projects, a beautiful sunset, or anything else that lifts our soul. Adolescents spend a lot of time together experiencing aesthetic intimacy, though observers may not recognize it over the pounding of the music.

In staying awake, it is vital to recognize what intimacy needs one has in these areas and to maintain the relationships necessary to fulfill them. Intimate relationships are the conduit to healing our childhood deprivations. They also lead us to deeper awareness of ourselves.

One other person or a partner is usually not enough to meet all our intimacy needs. Yet some of us may have been taught that they should. We needed only one person to fulfill us until the age of six months or so. When my primary partner can fulfill three or four of these areas in any given day, that is outstanding!

In maintaining healthy relationships with others, it is important that we have awareness of the value we place on our own intimacy needs. We then become responsible for managing these areas instead of waiting for someone to take care of us.

Guided Imagery on Self-Intimacy

Guided imagery involves putting yourself in a comfortable place, getting relaxed, and allowing your imagination to take the lead. Often times guided imagery is conducted by a trained facilitator who serves as a guide, speaks calmly, and helps explain a visualization process. The following is a guided imagery exercise I frequently use in class (and with myself) in order to promote greater awareness of intimacy needs, repressed feelings, and one's current general state of well-being.

I find my imagination works best in a relaxed or reclining state with very quiet music playing in the background. After I am relaxed I close my eyes and imagine myself sitting in a house with a basement door. I begin to realize that there are parts of me hiding in the basement. As I go down the stairs to visit with them, I see many aspects of me sitting on the floor. Some are angry, some are scared, and some go into hiding at seeing me. I then begin to visit with one of them at a time, trying to learn why they are hiding, and what happened to them. I am often surprised to find how many "children" are down there! One by one I ask what they need from me to feel safe enough to come out of hiding.

Many people find this to be a powerful exercise when they first do it and discover significant aspects of their identity in their basement. Some run into their shadow or an aspect of themselves they long ago rejected. Some find their defenseless hurts and disappointments. I often find my childlike nature, hiding from some aspect of life that I do not believe my adult-like self will protect me from, as she often does not acknowledge me under her defenses and intellect. What aspects of your being do you think have been stored in your basement for protection?

I find the basement a powerful metaphor for me regarding both my repressed feelings and thoughts. I repeatedly have tornado dreams when I rely heavily on defenses. In these dreams a tornado is usually chasing me. I've noticed that its size and the levels underground I must seek to be safe usually correspond to my use of denial and repression. Sometimes when I am in balance with myself,

I have the ability to stop hiding in the dream and stand up to the wind of the tornado and ask it why it is chasing me. At this point the tornado will always dissipate. Sometimes it will dissolve into a soft mist (like a Casper, the ghost cartoon character) and reveal what I am actually running from in my waking life!

CONCLUSION
EXPANDING CHOICE AND FREEWILL

We who lived in concentration camps can remember the men who walked through the huts comforting others, giving away their last piece of bread. They may have been few in number, but they offer sufficient proof that everything can be taken away from a man but one thing; the last of the human freedoms...to choose one's attitude in any given circumstances, to choose one's own way.
—Viktor Frankl *Man's Search for Meaning*

While this last section concludes the bulk of my written ideas, as with life, it really offers a momentary stop as we continue on our respective journeys. We considered how we fall asleep, waking up, and staying awake. These are related processes, all essential to realizing who we are becoming.

I would like to leave you with a few additional ideas to consider related to the important process of generating choices and exercising one's free will.

We begin life as wide-open beings ready to experience but not yet required to exercise choice. In fact, about the only thing we do is eat, sleep, and continue a never ending process of learning and growing. As you read, those around us—our parents, siblings, and other family members—have a tremendous impact on what we learn, the skills we develop to survive and thrive, and the choices we begin to make. This process tends to run as if on autopilot as we continue to age. We continue to be heavily influenced by others, including our school mates, our communities, our culture, and our society. And we react in ways that are consistent with what we are taught.

Sometimes we find that this more or less automatic process works just fine for us and we continue to progress through life. Maybe some of you reading this book realize that something may be missing or there may be something more to experience. You may have come to realize that something you were taught as fact or truth is really just someone else's opinion. Perhaps you started to question things when someone asked you what you thought about a subject and your response sounded just like your mother's. Perhaps you had reason to pause and reflect when you met a person who was different, unique, and didn't quite fit into the mold of how people are supposed to be. Maybe the mere passage of time has moved you to ask yourself, "What do I really think? What do I really feel? Who am I?"

This usually begins a process of learning at a richer and deeper level. In fact, interestingly enough, the process may also involve un-learning some of the things you have previously learned. This dynamic process, once started, is really difficult to arrest. It comes with twists and turns, ups and downs. Often we discover that things we felt were stable as a rock are very dynamic. This can lead to reassessing, more questions, additional learning, and an inevitable increase in understanding. Sometimes new learning can be difficult to accommodate. It involves change. Yet it is absolutely invigorating as we break the chains of formerly constraining thoughts, beliefs, fears, and anxiety.

As with so many of the examples and experiences discussed in the book, the process of staying awake is very personal. Gaining greater awareness arises from one's ability to create more options and choices. When we find ourselves under stress, it may see only one option. When I hear myself say, "only one option," I tell myself it cannot be true. I engage in a playful dialogue with my observing self to break the tension. "So you think that there is only one option?"

"Yes that is right," I respond, "only one option." And I clearly describe that option.

My observing self, who knows well my central tendency under stress, playfully suggests that there is at least one additional option and comments, "Well, I heard your option. "Why not just do the opposite? Wouldn't that be a second option? And if that option is too far from what you had in mind, couldn't you find a third or fourth option somewhere between?"

At this point I generally laugh at the creative approach that I (I mean, my observing self) has come up with and how stubborn I can be. I usually wrap up the conversation with my self by acknowledging, "You are right you obstinate soul, there is more than one option. In fact there are lots of options to consider."

Generating additional options provides a wonderful opportunity to exercise my free will. I find that considering options, which seek out balance (as in options away from extremes that often involve more reaction, rather than action), usually translate into choices that are healthier for me and those affected by my decisions. I believe this process is free will functioning in its highest form, from our unconstrained essence instead of our fears.

Life does not have to be so difficult and we do not have to accept this so-called noble truth to transcend it, if we simply wake up. We do not wake up by trying to save the world first. We wake up by restoring our essence of the self. Then and only then do we have the compassion or wisdom to save anything else.

Bibliography/Suggested Reading List

Beattie, Melody.. *Codependent No More*. Center City, MN: Hazelden, 1987.

Black, Claudia. *Don't Talk, Don't Trust, Don't Feel*. Center City, MN: Hazelden, 1987.

Black, Claudia. *Double Duty: Dual Dynamics Within the Chemically Dependent Home*. New York: Ballantine Books, 1990.

Black, Claudia. *Straight Talk from Claudia Black: What Recovering Parents Should Tell Their Kids About Drugs and Alcohol*. Center City, MN: Hazelden, 2003.

Cameron, Julia. *The Vein of Gold: A Journey to Your Creative Heart*. New York: Putnam, 1996.

De Mello, Anthony. *The Song of the Bird*. Garden City, NY: Image Books, 1984.

Frankl, Viktor E. *Man's Search for Meaning*. Boston: Beacon Press, 1963.

Gibran, Khalil. *The Prophet*. New York: A. A. Knopf, 1923.

Kaufman, Gershen. *Shame: The Power of Caring*. Cambridge, MA: Schenkman Pub. Co., 1980.

Miller, Alice. *The Drama of the Gifted Child*. New York: Basic Books, 1990.

Osho. *Awareness The Key to Living in Balance: Insights for a New Way of Living*. New York: St. Martin's Griffin, 2001.

Pearce, Joseph C. *Magical Child*. New York: Plume, 1992.

Satir, Virginia. *Peoplemaking*. Palo Alto, CA: Science and Behavior Books, 1972.

Schreiber, Flora R. *Sybil*. Chicago: Regnery, 1973.

Thoreau, Henry D., & Rogers, B. *Walden*. Cambridge: Riverside Press, 1889.

Wegscheider-Cruse, Sharon., & Cruse, Joseph. R. *Understanding Co-Dependency*. Deerfield Beach, FL: Health Communications, 1990.

Wegscheider, Sharon. *The Family Trap*. Rapid City, SD: Nurturing Networks, 1976.

Williamson, Marianne. *A Return to Love: Reflections on the Principles of "A Course in Miracles."* New York: HarperCollins, 1992.